MEMOIRS OF A DEPUTY CORONER:
The Case of Marilyn Monroe

Lionel Grandison Jr.
Samir Muqaddin

Table of Contents

Acknowledgements

Thanking those who have contributed to this story and in some ways to the completion of this book would take many pages, and we would still unintentionally neglect to name someone. But we would not feel this book is complete without furnishing a shortlist:

We are especially grateful to our loving soul mates, Chanelle, and Yvonne. It has been their undying support, encouragement, strength, comfort, and warmth that has sustained us all along.

To the third member of our team, Lionel Grandison II, we apologize for the tirades and arguments we had to put you through while writing this book. Thankfully, we can now go back to normal.

We are especially grateful to our editor, Amber Grandison, who rushed home after graduation from the University of California at Irvine to polish and push the manuscript toward publication.

Joining in to take up some of the slack is Crystal Jackson, Lance Grandison, Alithra "Tipy" Louda, Geoff Gilstrap, Cory Crismon, and Tony James Jr. Their efforts are all much appreciated.

Also included on the list are Veda James, Ora Hutchinson, Minnie Lee Williams, Romie "Bobby" James, and Frank & Lolita "Auntie" McCrimmon.

Last but not least, we humbly dedicate this book to all the people who have put their lives and reputations on the line to discover Marilyn's real cause of death, including Robert & Debra Slatzer, Jack Clemmons, and Jeanne Carmen.

From The Author

Most people grow up with an image of their parents that remains with them for a large part of their lives. It is imprinted upon us from the time of birth and quickly evolves into our reality. Then suddenly, one day after our parents have gotten older and usually we have too, like magic, you begin to see them differently. Sometimes it may be good and sometimes not so much, but it's always illuminating.

In 2010, I decided to write a book about my father's experiences with the case of Marilyn Monroe. My dad was the Los Angeles County Coroner's Deputy, who signed her death certificate for those of you who don't know. During his investigation, he witnessed a cover-up of epic proportions. He paid a considerable price because he discovered Marilyn's secret diary.

The decision to write this book was due to my father completing his memoirs. They included every detail he had ever written or investigated regarding Marilyn Monroe's case during the past 50 years. When he brought me his papers, I was stunned by the story he had told.

Although I'd grown up hearing about his ordeal and experienced the aftermath, many years had passed since the subject of Marilyn's death resurfaced. By then, I had been married for 20 years had two children of my own. My daughter was a junior in college with medical school in her sights, and my son was working with me in our family business. Neither of them knew the story of Marilyn Monroe, much less it involved their Grandfather. After reading my father's memoirs, I knew it was time for that to change.

It is difficult to explain the impact his memoirs had on me. When I began to read his innermost thoughts about Marilyn's case and how it impacted his life, almost inexplicably, something changed. I began to see my father differently and understand the man he truly was. His story was riveting, and when my reading was complete, I knew this information had to be published for all to see.

Before beginning to write this book, I shared the memoirs with some friends of mine in the entertainment industry. They were just as floored as I was. One of them later called and said he had a major Hollywood producer who wanted to make a film about my father's life. The producer, whose film credits included "The Butterfly Effect," starring Ashton Kutcher and "Lucky Number Slevin," starring Bruce Willis, invited my dad and me to his home in the Hollywood Hills. While there, he offered to purchase my dad's life-story rights.

At the time, he was in the middle of producing "The Rum Diaries," starring Johnny Depp. We signed the deal and later did a huge story with Variety Magazine about our upcoming movie. Ultimately, the producer encountered some difficulties and withdrew from the movie deal. Meanwhile, I began writing this book, spending long hours going through my dad's memoirs, and talking to him about the case of Marilyn Monroe.

His recollections and accounts about the people involved were mesmerizing. He provided in-depth details about the days following Marilyn's death and what transpired at the coroner's office. He talked about his relationships in 1962, with Los Angeles County Chief Medical Examiner, Theodore Curphey, and the man who performed the autopsy, Dr. Thomas Noguchi. My father personally knew nearly everybody involved with the official case.

He talked about being only 22 years old when he walked into the office that Sunday morning and being assigned her case. His memoirs thoroughly described the drama that followed, including finding her diary in the property recovered in from her house. Although I'd seen his diary notes before, subsequent years of his investigation made the information even more pertinent.

Interestingly enough, during my early twenties, I had encouraged my father to begin writing his memoirs. In fact, with my younger sister and brother, we started organizing all of his research papers, including the diary notes. We transferred nearly everything to floppy discs and made it available for whenever he decided to begin writing. That was the last time we talked about his memoirs.

Writing the book also reminded me of what our family endured during the historic 1982 District Attorney's Inquiry into Marilyn Monroe's death. Most people have never experienced what it feels like when the news media decides you're the hot story. During the 82' Inquiry, our neighborhood was under siege with news trucks and reporters hounding our house, as you'd never believe. They persistently asked questions, calling and harassing us, while making life miserable for everyone.

I didn't understand what was happening during that time. But after reading through the memoirs, my father explained details about that inquiry I never knew. He wrote about how Assistant District Attorney Ronald Carroll, tried to intimidate him and what he said during his interview with my father. My dad painted a picture most people never understood about the investigation, revealing how the DA's office wasn't trying to uncover the truth.

Ronald Carroll died not long after my father completed his memoir. The Los Angeles Times wrote an obituary story about him, describing the 82' inquiry and how my father's statements were the primary reason for launching the District Attorney's investigation. Although Carroll stayed with the ruling of Marilyn committing suicide, my father never waivered from his testimony and quest to discover truth.

After completing our book, a new light shined on what my amazing father went through. His struggles to reveal the truth about Marilyn Monroe's death have led me to believe my father, Lionel Grandison, is an American hero. My only hope now is that by reading the book, more people will understand his story, how he fought for Marilyn and the ultimate price he paid.

Preface

Throughout literary history, the old cliché "truth is stranger than fiction" is perhaps the most infamous. However, never in my wildest dreams did I think this oft-used term could describe fifty years of my life. My name is Samir Muqaddin, but at birth, it was Lionel Grandison.

The factual story I am about to present is compelling as any detective novel or Sci-Fi thriller. It covers my extraordinary experience with the life and death of a public figure who was perhaps the most well-known movie star ever.

The legend of Marilyn Monroe may well be Hollywood's biggest story. Her friends adored her, fans idolized her, and powerful men seemed drawn to her. However, to quote another cliché, "things were not as they seemed." Marilyn had secrets. She wrote about them in a little red book that I happened to read. I believe that she intended to reveal these secrets, but her lips were forever silenced one summer night in 1962 at her Los Angeles home.

As fate would have it, I crossed paths with Marilyn Monroe and her diary the day following her death. It would begin a chain of events that forever changed my life. What I read in that book and my firsthand involvement in the investigation has led me to tell this personal story over five decades in the making.

While investigating the circumstances surrounding her death, both as a public official and private citizen, my life became the target of those trying to cover up the truth. For many years I have been silent, but now I'm willing to tell my story one final time.

There has been a conspiracy to cover up the circumstances surrounding Marilyn's death for a half-century. Seemingly earnest law enforcement investigators, publicists, and politicians have informed the public that the presented evidence indicated suicide. With conviction, they passed on the information given by so-called medical experts, including the Los Angeles County Coroner, without ever presenting all the evidence. Their actions have left the task of revealing the ugly facts of the case to journalists and people like me.

I began organizing my memoirs and gathering my notes on Marilyn's diary in 1978. It started after meeting a journalist who encouraged me to come forward with my firsthand knowledge of what happened at the coroner's office. He held the belief that Marilyn was a murder victim and that government officials were involved. Together we would mount a challenging effort to re-open the case.

This book is my attempt to set the record straight on Coroner's Case# 81128. As a Deputy Coroner's Aide for the County of Los Angeles, I was assigned to assist the Medical Examiner in gathering all the necessary evidence to investigate Marilyn's cause of death. The question of

how she died has never received a reasonable answer, and
I   reluctantly   signed   her   death   certificate.

There was no conclusion as to what pills she took or who prescribed them. I have gathered all the evidence, along with everything I know about this case, and combined it with updated FBI and CIA disclosures. My goal is to shed new light on this 50-year old mystery.

In 2010, a new document was released under the Freedom of Information Act, verifying that the Central Intelligence Agency was bugging Marilyn's house the night she died. Since nearly 50 years had passed before the information was released, a valid explanation of the U.S. Government's involvement in Marilyn Monroe's death could still be a long time coming.

In Marilyn's writings and during my investigation, I discovered complications in her life that scared off the Los Angeles Police Department and county officials. These same complications were severe enough to get her killed.

The memoir I have written is a culmination of my life experiences and case research supported by eyewitness accounts, published works, and government documents. It is my personal story about the case of Marilyn Monroe. The only thing that remains is for you to sit down and digest it.

CHAPTER 1:
Introduction to a Conspiracy

I picked up the Los Angeles Times in 2010 and read that Ronald Carroll, a retired Los Angeles County District Attorney had died. He was involved in many high profile cases and headed a 1982 review of actress Marilyn Monroe's death in 1962. I discovered from the article that during a 33-year career in the District Attorney's office, beginning in 1966, Carroll also served as Chief Prosecutor in the highly publicized trial that resulted from a four-hour gun battle between the Black Panthers and police in 1969.

It was fascinating that the Los Angeles Times chose these two cases to highlight his career, as both required active concealment of facts to keep the truth from the public. However, for me, it was something much more personal. These two cases mirrored a 50-year reflection of my life and involvement with perhaps the most extensive cover-up of the 20th century. The article went on to say that in 1982 Carroll was assigned to conduct a "threshold inquiry" to determine whether a full-scale homicide investigation of Monroe's death was justified. The decision to investigate was due to charges by a former coroner's deputy, who said that a diary purportedly kept by Monroe had disappeared from the Coroner's office. He also alleged, "the diary contained the names of key government officials and conversations relating to sensitive government matters."

The Los Angeles Times article referred to the last official probe into the strange death of Marilyn Monroe. This inquiry resulted from my statements to Los Angeles County Officials that the actual cause of death was not correctly determined.

Assistant District Attorney Carroll interviewed me during his probe. I told him the Coroner's investigation into the cause of death had been a farce, and the diary described her involvement in many activities. Despite the testimony, Carroll said he did not find any credible evidence that the Coroners Office was ever in possession of a diary. He completely disregarded the fact that three other witnesses testified to seeing the book and other crucial evidence suggesting its existence. The Times reported, and Carroll concluded, that a murder of Monroe, fitting known facts of her death, would have required a massive conspiracy.

When the Los Angeles County District Attorney ignored the evidence and chose not to investigate Marilyn's death, they missed a unique opportunity. It was the last chance to collect sworn testimony from all the key witnesses who were still alive. As it turned out, this Inquiry, along with the other investigative probes, was part of the massive conspiracy to cover up evidence in the Marilyn Monroe case.

Twenty years earlier, the Los Angeles County Coroner and the Los Angeles Police Department had also covered-up evidence during their investigation. For them, the case was simply too hot to handle. From what we know now, they would've had to subpoena documents from the Federal Bureau of Investigation and Central Intelligence Agency, including sensitive notes and memos. They also would have needed to question a prestigious member of perhaps America's most powerful and influential family. Judging by their actions, they neither had the courage or determination for that.

All the information obtainable from those sources would have gone a long way toward clearing up the mystery surrounding Marilyn's death. Those investigations were part of an elaborate conspiracy that has baffled the public ever since that time.

The vision of what happened to Marilyn Monroe can only be reflections of the startling truth portrayed in a realistic elaboration of the known facts. It is hardly surprising that disseminating such information to the general public is apt to cause certain pessimism. The immediate reaction is that if any social or political problems existed, they would have been revealed by those best equipped for solving it.

To those who don't remember her, Marilyn Monroe was Hollywood. Fifty years after her death, she remains one of the most beloved and controversial women in history. To men, Marilyn was the ultimate sex symbol, and to women, either adored or despised. To Hollywood, she was always a headline for front-page cover stories in gossip magazines or major newspapers.

Since her death, her estate has made twenty times more money than she ever made in her life.

Only one of her films was a box office smash, but the camera always found her nonetheless. Her walk, smile, and appearance were her most significant assets. However, behind the bright lights, this brave woman had been lured into a cloak and dagger lifestyle.

The core of this story is a journal or diary allegedly written by Monroe, which in her own words she wrote accounts of the last ten or so years of her life. I got a glimpse of her complicated world after reading the diary at the Los Angeles County Coroner's Office the day after she died. During my investigation, a purse containing a little red book landed on my desk labeled "Marilyn Monroe property."

In that book, Marilyn kept a detailed description of events in her life, the centerpiece in this saga. The book disappeared from Los Angeles County Coroner's Office days after being brought in from her house and never recovered.

It seems incredible that we remember her as an emotionally disturbed, suicidal woman destined for this ending. Nothing in that diary gave me such an impression. If she was depressed or had entertained the idea of suicide, it was only out of fear of what she was involved in. The conspiracy to classify her as suicidal is a fragment of an overall plot by those obscuring the truth. Maybe she wrote her suicidal intentions in another book. There have been two or three other accounts of journals mentioned over the years, but I only saw this one.

The essence of her notes developed an intricate series of events that made me wonder if her death was the result of knowing too much. I witnessed a cover-up of the facts that not only affected the Coroner's investigation but other law enforcement agencies. Questions about her involvement with the Intelligence Community and what part the Kennedy White House played in this massive conspiracy to cover-up the truth still go unanswered. I feel strongly that a Coroner's inquest would have brought forth necessary evidence to determine the actual cause of death, forcing the police to investigate more thoroughly.

In my investigation, the facts never supported information authorities received from Marilyn's doctors, Ralph Greenson and Hyman Engelberg. In his professional opinion, Dr. Engelberg said it had been the pills he prescribed that caused Marilyn's death. Dr. Greenson, her psychiatrist, said Marilyn had been depressed and was suicidal.

The sworn depositions led to the readily accepted conclusion of her suicidal death. Still, these doctors were both guilty of misleading authorities. Evidence of a more sinister set of circumstances has emerged.

The Los Angeles Police Department used the doctor's statements to reach their final conclusion. The Coroner's ruling of Probable Suicide was enough for them to discount whatever other evidence made them uncomfortable.

While at the Coroner's Office, I had many conversations with Los Angeles County Coroner Dr. Theodore Curphey and Dr. Thomas Noguchi, who did the autopsy. Also, Dr. Ralph Abernathy, who did the toxicology test, the Suicide Investigation Team, and numerous police officers present at the crime scene. None of them could offer a credible answer as to what killed her.

Although Public officials were hesitant to get involved with the politics of Marilyn's death, it has now become apparent to me that the public has kept this story alive. For 50 years, they have questioned their picture of legal institutions as pursuers of justice, and the reality of deceitful collusion involving high officials. Such connivance discounts the value of life, particularly in the death of a universally loved personality like Marilyn Monroe.

In the context of public perception, even when the official investigation proclaimed suicide, it hardly changed American people's attitude. Their thirst for the truth has endured, inspiring numerous publishers, researchers, producers, journalists, and investigators to look for clues as to what really happened.

Now, who am I? Who is this man that spent almost all of his adult life answering questions and investigating the death of a Hollywood icon? In 1962, I was a happily married 22-year old man with three children and employed by the County of Los Angeles as a Deputy Coroner's Aide. I had transferred to the Coroner's office as a supervising clerk in 1960, promoted in 1961 to this higher position. My job at the Los Angeles County Coroner's Office was to investigate deaths in the County and ensure the upholding of all State of California laws.

I had taken advantage of the new hiring policies put in place following World War II. Color or race could no longer be an issue in civil service hiring. Minorities could pass an exam and get placed on a list that guaranteed consideration for employment within the County, City, State, and Federal Governments. Jobs like Coroner's Deputy were now available if you were qualified. If you placed number one on the test exam, it was hard to justify turning you down.

For me, coming out of the bus boycotts, sit-ins, and freedom rides of the 1950s, it was important for all Americans to receive equal protection under the law. Working for the Los Angeles County Coroner's Office was a privilege taken very seriously. I understood the significance of that position and embraced that responsibility. For me, in this new era, things were not going to be business as usual in County Government when it came to the ordinances governing the rights of citizens.

So when the Coroner, Police, District Attorney, or any other agency with a perceived sense of power came to me with something outside the legal parameters, I called them out. Never did I go along with something that wasn't ethical. My reputation developed as a straight shooter who would follow the letter of the law, even when it was not popular.

Recognizing my thorough and fair approach, department supervisors began using me to clear up issues in the minority community. Cases, where families fought over who was in charge burials or had disagreements with the Coroner's findings, were sent to me.

During that time, African American and Latino mortuaries received unfair treatment by a discriminatory tradition of not designating them as Coroner's representatives. This practice created a different standard of rules and placed these minority-owned mortuaries at a competitive disadvantage. Whenever they complained, they sent them to me.

In the Investigation Department of the Coroner's Office, about six or more deputies received assigning to high-profile cases needing extensive police investigation. It required working closely with the Autopsy Surgeons. Other Deputies worked our first-call desk, gathering medical information and police reports for the files. All of us signed death certificates once the cases were closed. In the medical department, there was a pool of stenographers, some laboratory chemists, file clerks, and another 20 or more Deputies who picked up the bodies and gathered evidence from the scene.

The Chief Medical Examiner/Coroner was Dr. Theodore Curphey. He was one of the highest appointed officials in the County of Los Angeles. His duties included:

1. Responsibility for determining the cause of death of any person who didn't have an attending physician.
2. Investigating any death with a traumatic injury caused by accident or at the hands of another.
3. Investigating all homicides and suicides.

To reach a verdict in matters of death, the Coroner could call upon numerous resources. These included all police departments, the L.A. County District Attorney, Los Angeles City Attorney, and even State or Federal government agencies. The Coroner had the power to convene an inquest and subpoena witnesses to testify. His staff was responsible for assuring the accuracy of medical facts, police evidence, and proper identification of the deceased. The most important aspect of the first hours or days was notifying the next of kin for information and burial. The morgue was not a place where relatives wanted their loved ones to be.

Most of the cases were typical with identifiable causes of death submitted by attending physicians. However, murders, suicides, accidental deaths, and traffic fatalities were more challenging. All police departments in Los Angeles County provided detectives to investigate the facts for the Coroner and scrutinize medical opinions that didn't agree with the circumstances.

With Beverly Hills and Hollywood being part of Los Angeles County, we often dealt with deaths involving the rich and famous. These cases usually involved high-powered attorneys and investigators, who were concerned about estate or insurance issues. So whenever the story began getting a little complicated, often, a spin-doctor was busy at work.

My personal experiences with the Marilyn Monroe case come from the official Coroner's Office investigation, District Attorney, Grand Jury Inquiries, and numerous television interviews. They include years of researching government disclosures, journalistic reports, and newspaper accounts of the facts. It adds to what is now an extensive list of investigations by numerous journalists and researchers who have examined the suicide question.

Although my observations initially did not get taken seriously, recent CIA disclosures have verified many of my accounts. Certain things that Marilyn addressed in her diary received proof to have transpired. So we can assume most, if not all, of her written passages possessed veracity. With that said, it wasn't until many years later that I began to realize the social significance of the words.

In the mid-seventies, I finally met someone else who had seen the book and held extensive knowledge of Marilyn's case. The information he shared allowed me to put faces to many names that Marilyn had written about and connected details from her case like never before.

This person was journalist Robert Slatzer, one of the foremost authorities on the subject of Marilyn Monroe. Together, we spent many years of investigative research uncovering facts about Marilyn's death and validating what was in the diary.

Since that time, there have been press conferences and numerous television, radio, newspaper, and magazine interviews. During these occasions, I have always expressed my argument against the suicide claim. My story even got told to the Los Angeles County Board of Supervisors, who then recommended a grand jury investigation of her death.

Over the years, I have heard and witnessed many unsettling accounts of those who reported what happened. Being the Coroner's deputy who investigated Marilyn's case has afforded me many advantages. I observed many of the events that occurred after she died, so my perspective may be more creditable. Above all, the most compelling circumstance about my story is the journal or diary allegedly written by Marilyn Monroe. During my investigation, I maintained possession of her official case files and logged her property. Over two days, I read the journal and took notes to aid my investigation.

In my testimony over the years, I have never gone into detail about what was in the book because it was incriminating, intimidating, and politically sensitive. Although it provided a long list of associates and suspects, the diary never directly stated who killed her. The District Attorney never wanted to talk about the names mentioned in the journal. Though many people claimed to have seen Marilyn's diary, it never became public.

I cannot one hundred percent verify she wrote it. However, I did compare it with other handwriting samples in her property. One of my investigative responsibilities at the Coroner's Office was to compare suicide notes with other documents written by the deceased person. Her driver's license signature, papers in her purse, and legal documents I was able to obtain led me to believe Marilyn legitimately wrote the diary.

The diary told an intriguing tale of what she was involved in. It revealed who she was involved with and how she felt about it. As I looked at her passages, I was particularly impressed with how Marilyn kept her thoughts intact during an ordeal that would have made most of us cringe. If you had the CIA, FBI, Secret Service, Mafia, and the Kennedy family mad enough to kill you, what would you do?

It has taken me a long time to articulate a valid interpretation of what I read. Marilyn's observations needed to be researched and taken seriously for what it suggests about twentieth-century America. Many other journalists concur with the accounts in the diary and have verified her involvement with the intelligence community.

Much has happened to me since reading the diary and being involved in her official case, providing all the real-life drama one could ever need. I have been threatened, harassed, embarrassed, charged with a crime, and had my marriage destroyed because of what I learned and my overall connection with the Marilyn Monroe investigation. Despite these difficult situations, I knew my resolve and that my good character would see me   through   if   the   truth   was   known.

CHAPTER 2:
Sign of the Times

First, let me set the stage with my assessment of what was happening in America following World War II. Two movements, destined to change America forever, were starting to take root. During the late forties and early fifties, almost every federal agency had become involved in the anti-Communist and anti Civil Rights crusade. The actions of the federal government helped to forge and legitimize the severe violations of civil liberties that characterized the Senator Joe McCarthy era. It was a cold war period that fueled fears of widespread communism in America.

In this atmosphere, our nation instituted the Central Intelligence Agency to create a fully functional intelligence office. The CIA was responsible for coordinating the nation's intelligence activities and correlating, evaluating and disseminating intelligence affecting national security. Their methods ranged far beyond international intelligence gathering. Ultimately, the organization began domestic operations that would exceed its congressional mandate.

The media was the government's partner, primarily because it amplified messages that came from Washington. After all, much of the news I heard on the radio or saw in the newspapers only reported the government's doings. Presidential orders, congressional hearings, and criminal prosecutions all told stories that helped fuel the attacks on American citizens' constitutional rights.

It was this world Marilyn Monroe found herself in during the early fifties. Ironically, Marilyn's writings related the extent of Communist penetration in Hollywood as she wrote about the number of Communists she had come to know. One of her husbands, writer Arthur Miller, was considered the greatest dramatist of the 20th century and a known Communist sympathizer. The House Un-American Activities Committee would investigate him during its investigation of Communist activity within the film industry.

As the middle of the decade arrived, a rising challenge based on the age-old problem of racial prejudice would soon dominate the national stage. The Federal Bureau of Investigation, led by Agency Director J. Edgar Hoover, would actively become involved. Hoover accused Civil Rights activists, Labor leaders, and Hollywood writers of being communists for challenging the laws of the land.

When political trials and other traditional legal modes of control failed to counter the growing movements and even helped to stimulate them, the FBI and police moved outside the law. They resorted to the secret and systematic use of fraud, deceit, and force to sabotage constitutionally protected political activity.

The former General of the Army, Dwight D. Eisenhower was elected President to lead the country through these difficult times. As he left office, he said to beware of these agencies and the military complex because the power and money bestowed upon them could corrupt the country.

Meanwhile, America's middle-class citizens began to mobilize with their agenda. Organized Labor unions began to provide an economic base for this new class of citizens who wanted inclusion in the American dream. The unions, run by a seedy group of people who included Organized Crime figures, helped them negotiate wages with the corporate power structure. After years of frustration since the turn of the century, workers didn't care who they partnered with to achieve their goals.

Congressional committees were empowered to fight the labor movement under the banner of resisting communist and socialist domination of the world. The FBI maintained this position while serving legal indictments against Americans Hoover called socialist instigators.

During the decade, Former United States Ambassador Joe Kennedy introduced his two sons, John and Robert, to the political landscape. His sons brought a new image to politics, young, good-looking, articulate, Harvard educated, and someone whom with the new middle class could identify.

John Kennedy served in the House of Representatives (1947-1953) and the U.S. Senate (1953-1960). He gained national prominence while serving on the Senate Select Committee on Improper Activities in the Labor and Management Field. This powerful Committee held public hearings to investigate corruption in American labor unions.

Robert Kennedy made a name for himself as the Senate Labor Rackets Committee's chief counsel while trying to indict Jimmy Hoffa. In a dramatic scene, Kennedy squared off with the Teamsters union President during the antagonistic argument that marked Kennedy's introduction to mainstream America. Kennedy left the Committee to run his brother's successful presidential campaign.

John was already having an affair with Marilyn when he was elected President. During that time, she became actively involved with CIA activities both in America and abroad. Marilyn was young, ambitious, and talented, but even these qualities would not last long in this dangerous environment. For that matter, neither did the Kennedy's. As fate would have it, all three became destined for assassination.

Both John and Robert were sexually and politically involved with Monroe. They took her to meetings where discussions of sensitive government matters took place. It placed her in an inescapable dangerous environment during the last two years of her life.

After reading Marilyn's diary and investigating her case, I found myself also unable to escape. When the wrath of the higher-ups came down upon me for my unyielding determination to discover the real cause of death, my whole world turned into a nightmare.

I was a young African-American charged with the responsibility of gathering and verifying the circumstances surrounding her death. Although this strange case unfolded right in front of my eyes, I never saw it coming. Little did I know, or could have imagined, how that would impact the rest of my life.

Many have tried to tell the Marilyn story. Some good, some bad, some self-serving, some helpful, some Kennedy influenced, and some CIA inspired. The problem was that many readers would perhaps be inclined to see the works as just another conspiracy theory or a typical look into the life of a troubled Hollywood personality.

At this time, I will take my turn explaining what happened to Marilyn, what she wrote in her diary, and why the public never saw the hidden details of her death. It should cause you to think about America's laws, politics, democracy, national security, the superrich, middle class, and overall national character. If not, you will have missed the broader significance of my experience. I'm also going to relate some of the inexplicable things that happened to me just because I crossed paths with Marilyn Monroe and that bleeping diary.

So in the words of a brilliant writer, I remember it as though it was yesterday.

CHAPTER 3:
One Day at the Office

On Sunday, August 5, 1962, I was working the weekend shift at the Los Angeles County Coroner's Office. It was about a thirty-five-minute drive from my house in the San Fernando Valley to downtown Los Angeles. There was little or no traffic on the freeway, so I remember coming into the parking lot in a good mood about ten minutes to eight. The office was in the Hall of Justice, which also housed the Los Angeles County Sheriff and District Attorney.

As I walked in, Deputy Coroner's Aide Albert Stiller informed me our supervising Deputy, Phillip Schwartzberg, had assigned me a hot case. He said it was on my desk. Stiller, who would work the Sunday shift with me, was a 15-year veteran of the Coroner's Office and very knowledgeable about procedures. Phil, our immediate boss, had worked for the County 25 years. He called every, and I do mean every morning at 5:00 AM to give assignments for homicide and other high profile cases.

As I remember, there were about ten or fifteen new cases that night, but figured if Schwartzberg had singled out this particular case, it needed the most attention. Deputy Cronkright had received the first report of the death of Marilyn Monroe from Dr. Ralph Greenson and Dr. Hyman Engelberg, sometimes between 4 and 5 AM. Armand

De La Rosa, one of the clerks who handled public inquiries, hung up the phone and said:

"This Marilyn Monroe thing is already crazy. I just came in today to clear some of my cases, and within 30 minutes, at least twenty-five people have called to inquire about her death. You see those lights blinking on the phone? Well, they are all calling about Marilyn. I'm going back home. Good luck to you, Lionel, and whoever else is working today."

Armand and I were the youngest employees in the office and had competed for the Deputy position I held. Most of the employees appreciated the long-term job security in the Coroner's Office and the sense of doing something for society. It had been eight years since a job title opened up. Following orders was the only thing required for everyone who worked in the office.

Sitting down at my desk that Sunday morning, the paperwork revealed the startling news. The police were reporting the actress died of an apparent drug overdose. Deputy Cronkright had written that 20th Century Fox Studio signed a release of Marilyn's body, saying they could handle the burial. However, removal of her body still required approval by the Coroner's Office.

The Studio and her doctors told our office it was a common drug overdose and asked could we release the body to Westwood Memorial Park Mortuary. As the Deputy in charge, it was my call. It was common practice to deputize a Mortuary to act on behalf of the Coroner. However, the circumstances must completely rule out the need for a complete autopsy with organ examination—moreover, the possibility of death at the hands of another.

With high profile cases like these, there generally comes a high degree of scrutiny, so I picked up the phone and called Marilyn's house. Police detectives were still at the scene, and lead investigator Sergeant R.E. Byron took my call. I told him there was additional information needed before we could release her remains. He told me that her body was already en route to Westwood mortuary. When I asked who authorized its release, Byron told me to hold for a moment. After returning a few minutes later, he reluctantly stated,

"Mrs. Monroe's remains were authorized for release by Peter Lawford, her friend, and 20th Century Fox, her employer."

Thinking that a little odd, I replied, "Who is the next of kin responsible for her burial?"

Apparently stumped by my question, the officer replied, "There were no known relatives present."

In a death such as this, California State Law prohibited the release of a body without next of kin authorization. Thanking the officer, I hung up the phone and immediately called Westwood Mortuary, ordering them to return Marilyn's remains to the house.

We then dispatched Coroner's Deputies to bring her downtown to the Hall of Justice for further investigation. The Coroner's representatives asked police for information regarding the doctors who reported the case or any extenuating circumstances. They also inquired about any suicide note, witness statements, pill bottles, prescriptions, and names of relatives at the house.

The case had begun rather strangely with LAPD and a reputable mortuary trying to remove her body. Despite thinking this was odd, I never would have envisioned this taking almost 50 years to investigate. But, as I found out later, the Coroner's Office turned out to be part two of the cover-up and would take place on my watch. There would be many other cover-ups to follow.

Previous experience with high profile cases had taught me that the scrutiny that parallels these investigations could make or break your future in this office. Months earlier, I was working the graveyard shift and received a call from a California Highway Patrol officer who said comedian Ernie Kovacs had died in an automobile accident. Kovacs was a Las Vegas headliner, who also had an Emmy nominated network television series in his resume. He died when his car crashed in the hills above Sunset Boulevard in Hollywood.

Pierce Brothers Mortuary was already there with a pre-need authorization from the family to remove the body. A pre-need is a funeral arrangement made by a person before their death. For me, this was always a red flag. It meant that someone had notified a mortuary before they had contacted the Coroner in an automobile fatality. Although common in a natural death, when a police agency responsible for the investigation calls the mortuary first, it is not proper. He went on to say that no one else was involved, and no alcohol was detected.

The Officer ordered me to note his conclusions on my report, which led me to determine the case was shaky. I told the officer we would dispatch Coroner's representatives to pick up the remains and inform the mortuary they could pick up Mr. Kovacs downtown. He vehemently protested my decision, but as a Coroner's representative, I always had authority in accident cases.

The next morning Kovacs' wife, singer Edie Adams, and actor Jack Lemmon were awaiting Dr. Curphey when he entered the office. Curphey, who arrived a little earlier than usual, looked at me when he walked in and said,

"Don't go home yet. We need to talk."

After he met with the others, Curphey called me to his office and questioned my judgment in handling the case. He said when police tell you everything is alright in a high profile case, consider it fact and follow their advice.

The Kovacs case was my first experience with intimidation while employed as a Los Angeles County Deputy Coroner. Curphey was trying to hinder my investigation of the facts with fear of external pressure from those in powerful places. It wouldn't be the only time. A few days later, the toxicology report showed double the amount of alcohol in the blood allowable under state law. When I presented these results to Dr.

Curphey, his response was, "Don't ever question my authority again."

Information later arrived from an insurance company, investigating a million-dollar double indemnity policy. However, it contained a clause stating no payment would transpire if Kovacs died from the result of an alcohol-related incident. This case also taught me that Millions of dollars were involved in these investigations. There is always more than what appears on the surface. I'm sure Mrs. Kovacs and a few others hated me for the rest of their lives.

By the time Marilyn's body got downtown, the office was frantic with phone calls. Newspapers from around the world wanted to know if her death was a suicide, as reported. Fox Studios and LAPD were already issuing press releases and holding press conferences describing her death as a suicide. I spent most of the afternoon on the phone, telling people we didn't have any information, and that her cause of death was pending the autopsy. You should have heard some of the things they said.

Finally, Coroner's representative Danbacker, who had picked up the body from the house, brought the medical information and personal property to my desk. Fox Studios couldn't produce a document with her signature on it that authorized them to handle funeral arraignments. I asked him if the police knew of any next of kin. He told me she apparently had a mother alive in a sanitarium, but no husband, no kids, and no other known family members.

Danbacker said there was no suicide note, but noticed that she had died much earlier than reported. Someone had forcibly opened a filing cabinet containing some of her papers. The housekeeper, Eunice Murray, said there was no will found. Marilyn's property consisted of a purse with a wallet, some charge cards, about $30 in cash, and a middle-sized book or journal. There was some jewelry, receipts, prescription containers, and a paper flyer announcing a press conference.

Looking through her property, I picked up the book and commenced my search for anything that would reveal an executor or next of kin. It appeared to be a diary about the size of a notebook. I opened the cover and began to read, trying to find anything that would assist in my investigation.

The opening page simply stated:

"This is for all the people who ever called me a dumb blond. I may be insecure, but not stupid. I only want to twinkle."

Those beginning words were striking but didn't nearly prepare me for the intellectual nature of the book. As I began scanning through it, some fascinating entries appeared on almost every page. I found several phone numbers without names or addresses associated with them. It didn't take me long to realize the unique nature of this book.

As I continued thumbing through the pages, it became impossible to ignore the depth of this book. It contained names straight out of the headlines of the national newspapers. There were enough hot entries for all the Hollywood gossip magazines to fill their pages. I saw notes referring to President Kennedy, the FBI, and even people she referred to as "the spy boys." I noticed words such as communist, assassination, Castro, and even Jimmy Hoffa.

On that day, it was difficult to concentrate on the explosiveness of what I was reading. The phone lines were blowing up, and things around the office were completely in disarray. Members of the press were everywhere, clamoring for what was turning out to be the story of the year. I decided to log the contents of her purse and put the property in the safe. My shift was ending soon, and it had been a long day. I made some notes for Monday, cleared up my desk, and went home.

When I arrived home, the neighborhood was abuzz with the news of Marilyn's death. My wife said all of our friends, who knew I worked at the Coroner's Office, were calling to get the inside story. The general public idolized Marilyn Monroe. From what I had read in her notes, the private sector as well.

I remember sitting on the couch and telling my wife about the diary and what I read. Her reaction was predictable. She said, "Are you serious?"

I told her yes and mentioned more about the book. She just looked at me. At that moment, I remember my son Lance, crying, and she picked him up. I'll never forget the look in her eyes as she held our child. She said,

"That book sounds like trouble. Trouble for you and trouble for us. Those are other people's problems. Do you really want to get involved? The President, communist, and FBI? I think you should just forget about it and pretend you never saw the book.

I knew she was right. That book was trouble, but what else could I do? I replied to her,

"Babe, I really don't know what to think, but it's my job to investigate. You can be sure a lot of people don't want this information made public. There are some prominent names written there, but I don't even know if any of this stuff is true. The strangest thing is that they tried to take the body. One thing I know is that I have a job to do. Tomorrow will be one hell of a day, and I'm sure Dr. Curphey will have something to say about me bringing in the body."

Monday morning traffic was back to normal, bumper to bumper. The travel time was now over an hour, but it gave me time to reflect on what I had seen at the Hall of Justice. When I first came to the Coroner's Office in 1960, my responsibility was to deal with the public inquiries and keep an up-to-date log on the status of open investigations. Now that I was a deputy, my responsibilities were more detailed.

The hot case of that time was George Reeves. Reeves was the actor that played Superman in the hit television series, *"The Adventures of Superman."* Many people were unhappy with the ruling of "indicated suicide", in Reeves' death, including his mother, Helen Besselo. She was desperately trying to convince everyone that someone murdered her son. Mrs. Besselo came in or called every week for a year, trying to get Dr. Curphey to convene a Coroner's inquest or change his ruling of suicide.

Unsure how to handle the situation, I went to Dr. Curphey's office for an official briefing about this sensitive case's status. Curphey was handling all inquiries for Reeves's death, and he advised me on how to answer her questions.

Dr. Curphey explained that Reeves' family had exhumed his body, and paid a pathologist for a second autopsy, while quickly commissioning their independent investigation. Curphey said our official position was "the Coroner's Department was standing by its ruling. We based it on our autopsy findings and the Los Angeles Police Department's investigation." He added there would not be any inquest scheduled. Nevertheless, Mrs. Besselo called almost every day, and office personnel passed the calls along to me as advised.

Her persistence led me to look through Reeves' official coroner files, where I discovered some interesting facts about his case. It seemed the deputy, who investigated the death, had been extremely quick to rule it a suicide. The police report said when they arrived, Reeves was lying naked on his bed, dead of a single gunshot wound to the right temple. The autopsy report indicated that there were no powder marks found on Reeves' body, and he had several fresh bruises.

Mrs. Besselo told me that during their investigation, private detectives uncovered mountains of evidence that did not quite match up with the Coroner's ruling of suicide. Among some of the mysterious facts was that no fingerprints found on the gun, leaving the possibility it was wiped clean. They found a spent shell casing underneath Reeves' body, which is very unusual. The locations of the entrance and exit wounds did not line up with the path of the bullet. Its entrance into the wall indicated this.

Regardless of whether or not he killed himself, it was evident that Reeves' death was never properly investigated. Private investigators claimed that police detectives received pressure to make it an "open and shut" case.

In 1961, after I became a deputy, Dr. Curphey ordered Reeves' body exhumed and cremated without his mother's approval, forever destroying whatever evidence was left behind. When Mrs. Besselo was informed and presented with the remains, she became severely depressed, dying a few years later.

This ordeal became my first experience involving an unsolved Hollywood mystery but certainly not the last. According to the official Coroner's findings, George Reeves had committed suicide, and the matter was closed.

Meanwhile, on the car radio, news of Monroe's death was on almost every station. As I got off the freeway, there seemed to be a lot of activity on the streets. In 1962, there were newspaper stands at every major intersection downtown. Men were coming up to cars, selling daily news. That morning they were screaming at the top of their lungs,

"Marilyn Monroe Found Dead!"

"Marilyn Monroe Commits Suicide!"

As I walked into the office that morning, it started to unfold in front of my very eyes. The typical laid back style of a somber Coroner's office had transformed into a frantic pace led by people who thought they were at the New York Stock Exchange. They were standing at the counter, shouting, "Is Marilyn Monroe really here, and can we view the body?"

Stiller was talking on the phone. He called out to me,

"Lionel, I'm glad you're here. I've got the New York Times on the phone, and they are asking if we are carrying her death as a homicide or suicide?"

I walked over to Phil Schwartzberg at the supervisor's desk and asked him had there been any updates. Phil said,

"We are waiting for word from the lab, but the police say suicide. Your job is getting her buried. We'll let the police handle the investigation."

After hanging up the phone, Stiller walked over and said,

"There were two men here about six this morning looking for you. They didn't identify themselves, but some of the guys from the autopsy room said they were Secret Service Agents. They were looking through some papers on your desk and for something in the medical department. Maybe some prescription bottles."

Although I couldn't determine what they were looking for on my desk, my thoughts went immediately to Marilyn's diary. After all, I had seen the President's name inside it. But how would they have known I had the book? The only other person who saw it was Danbacker.

I soon discovered the Secret Service had also been in the autopsy room. Maybe they were there to question him and his partner about what they had recovered from the house. Not sure of what to think, I resumed my investigation, but the depth of the case was quickly becoming a reality.

I went over to Deputy Lester Goldberg's desk, who was the investigator that usually handled high profile cases. He had ten years investigating Coroner cases and all the contacts in the city. Goldberg wore tailor-made suits, had a USC degree, and was said to have come from a well-connected family. People from around the country called him for official information from the Coroner office regarding complicated legal matters.

Goldberg was usually very well informed, so I asked him what he knew about Marilyn's case. He told me she was married to Joe DiMaggio and Arthur Miller but wasn't sure if she was legally divorced. Goldberg was already in contact with Marilyn's lawyer and heard there was something strange about her death. He didn't want to discuss it right then but emphasized we should go over it later, maybe during lunch.

Finally, arriving at my desk, I discovered a note from, you guessed it, Dr. Curphey, who wanted to see me about Marilyn's case. Also, the toxicology lab wanted more information from the physicians regarding prescription label discrepancies on the pill bottles Danbacker had brought in.

Walking down that long hall to Dr. Curphey's office was always an eerie experience. The sound of your shoe heels would echo like in a Hollywood horror movie.

I was always anxious about meeting with Dr. Curphey. He was a big man who was very imposing and maintained a frown on his face.

Highly respected in the pathology community, Curphey had a reputation for not caring what the public thought or anyone else. For that reason, controversy seemed to follow him. He always seemed very mysterious. None of us employees at the Coroner's Department ever looked forward to being in his office. It usually meant we were receiving a lecture because he was unhappy with our work.

When I arrived, he was sitting at his desk with Becker, his administrative assistant. Becker was second in command and oversaw all legal matters for the Coroner's office. As I walked in, it was noticeable neither of them was happy. Curphey then sternly stated,

"Hope you realize the kind of pressure you put on this office with your rash decisions. This case shouldn't have been difficult because it was an obvious suicide. Now everybody is breathing down my neck for information, and I don't need this crap. I'm assigning the Suicide Investigation Team to the case, so get them anything they need. Let's bring this to a quick conclusion, understand?"

Working hard to get where I was, it was always tough for me to accept people speaking harshly to me. However, I simply nodded yes to Dr. Curphey. I asked him if there would be an inquest or an LAPD homicide investigation. Still speaking sternly, he replied, "No." I walked out of his office. Outside, two FBI officials were waiting to see him. Having worked with them on several occasions, I nodded and went to the lab.

Dr. Ralph Abernathy was in charge of the Medical Department. He was responsible for toxicology, retrieving samples, conducting chemical tests, and overseeing microscopic examinations. Abernathy had taken her first blood sample and found no poison or traces of other medication that Marilyn could have swallowed to contribute to her death. He advised me to send another deputy to her house and call the police to see if they found any information on other prescription containers.

Associated Press, United Press International, and the rest of the print media pool were still milling around the office looking for information regarding the case. Rumors circulated among the reporters about Marilyn's death, including whispers of Robert Kennedy's involvement and a press conference she had scheduled. Of course, Marilyn Monroe was a hot topic around the office.

I hadn't released any information on what was in her property, like the diary or press release. There was a case to wrap-up, and my investigation was still incomplete, with pressure continuing to mount. I had Danbacker return to the house and bring back every prescription bottle he could find.

When I got back to my desk, I called Sergeant Jack Clemmons of the Los Angeles Police Department, the first officer at the scene. He informed me he was no longer on the case but did give me some information on Marilyn's business agent, Inez Melson. I asked Sgt. Clemmons if he knew whom the current detectives in charge were, but he didn't know. That became a theme for the LAPD as her investigation went on. No one ever knew who was in charge of investigating this case.

When I contacted Melson, she said that Marilyn's mother, Gladys Pearl Monroe, was committed to a sanitarium with mental problems. She didn't know of any other relatives. Melson also informed me that she thought there was a will.

It appeared as if only a will covering her estate or identifying someone who could handle her affairs would solve my problem. I pulled her property out and began to look for anything in the book that would reveal an executor. Truth be told, I wanted another look at her journal anyway, to see what information was really in there. This time I took notes.

CHAPTER 4:
The Little Red Book

The first 15 or 20 pages seemed to be recollections of her early involvement with specific people. These were long passages that took up full pages. As I began glancing through the journal, it became increasingly evident that Marilyn was involved in much more than movies. Page after page contained references to communist and different socio-political organizations. She was writing about intelligence agencies, using coded names, and recounting some incredible experiences. The first thing I discovered was her relationship with the United States Government.

She wrote:

"The FBI wanted me to do something for America. They sent Iron Bob to ask me if Arthur was a Communist. When I told him we weren't that close, he laughed and said you could get closer. He told me I should talk to Paula."

According to her journal, Washington had recruited talent from far and wide for its crusade against communism. During that time, I had no idea who Iron

Bob or Paula was. However, I knew Marilyn had been married to Arthur Miller. That story was big news, and Lester Goldberg had reminded me about it earlier. However, it wasn't until years later that I would discover these other identities.

As it turned out, I later identified Iron Bob as Robert Maheu, an agent of the Federal Bureau of Investigation. He seemingly was the first to approach Marilyn. Maheu was a former World War II Super Spy, who had posed as a Nazi sympathizer during the war. He also contracted with the Central Intelligence Agency doing assignments when the agency could not officially be involved.

Paula turned out to be actor Lee Strasberg's wife. She was also Marilyn's acting coach. The Government had blacklist Paula Strasberg as a communist. Apparently, she had some type of connection with the Bureau. According to FBI disclosures, Maheu was very effective in setting up covert operations such as this. It seems Maheu asked Marilyn to get information on Arthur Miller's alleged communist activities. Strasberg coached her through the process.

According to Marilyn, Maheu was keeping records of Miller's social and political activities.

There was an ongoing investigation into his association with groups making public statements against the government and its anti-communist blacklist.

She wrote:

"Iron Bob wanted the names of people with us during social engagements and information on Arthur's meetings with the American Labor Party and the ACLU."

Even during my younger years, I was always very socially and politically conscious. My grandparents were among the first African-American homeowners in the San Fernando Valley of Southern California. My grandfather was a Military veteran, construction worker, and part of the Union movement in the African-American and Latino communities.

Seeing Marilyn write about these highly charged subjects fascinated me. Was it possible that this blonde-bombshell Hollywood starlet was involved with these types of activities? Coincidently or not, Marilyn Monroe's movie career suddenly went into another gear during this time.

On New Year's Eve 1955, Marilyn signed a new contract with 20th Century Fox Studios to make four films over seven years. She formed Marilyn Monroe Productions, which received $100,000, plus a share of profits for each film.

In addition to allowing her to work for other studios, Monroe had the right to reject any script, director, or cinematographer that she did not approve. Before signing this deal, Marilyn's typical pay for a movie was only about $18,000.

We know that Hollywood was reeling with investigations by the House Un-American Activities Committee into certain actors and writers. When the government accused you of being a communist in the motion picture business, your ability to get a job or finance a film went downhill. Still, if they needed your help, the sky was the limit. With this power, it would have been easy for the FBI to get Studios to cooperate, sign Marilyn to a lucrative new deal, and cast her in some key roles.

Marilyn wrote in-depth pages about Arthur Miller and how the FBI played a central role early in their relationship. Iron Bob's name repeatedly occurred in this part of her writings.

Later she wrote:

"After we were married, Arthur said he wanted me to go to Russia with him. It sounded exciting, but when Iron Bob got wind of it, he told me I was getting in too deep."

Why was Iron Bob concerned about Marilyn getting in too deep? Was he apprehensive about her relationship with Miller? According to F.B.I records, Miller did ask her to go to the Soviet Embassy and apply for a visa. He wanted her to get a first-hand look at who the socialists were. The fact that the government knew Miller had asked Marilyn to go gives credence to her accounts in the book.

Arthur Miller was one of the nation's leading activists. He had recently written a Broadway play called "The Crucible," produced as a statement against McCarthyism when the US Government blacklisted accused communists. During that time, the U.S. House of Representatives had an investigative branch called the House Un-American Activities Committee. They were targeting and blacklisting writers who had written controversial books and screenplays about America. They subpoenaed Miller to appear in front of the Committee.

On one page I read:

"Paula and Lee told Arthur to come clean with the Committee, but he said he would not sell out his friends. Don't know why I gave that information. Guess I could be considered a sellout."

Apparently, just before his appearance in front of the House Un-American Activities Committee, Lee and Paula Strasberg had suggested that he go as a "friendly" witness, something that Paula herself had done several years earlier.

It seemed as though Marilyn began to second-guess her role in gathering information for the FBI. I don't think she ever thought it they'd use it in court against Miller. I believe that Maheu and Strasberg convinced Marilyn they were investigating other people and organizations. However, the House Un-American Activities Committee still subpoenaed Miller.

Arthur Miller was found guilty of Contempt of Congress for not naming some suspected communist writers he met with during that time.

Marilyn wrote:

"The war against communism tore our industry apart. I'm sorry they used me to get him."

I remember visiting Los Angeles City College in the late fifties while preparing to enroll. It was surprising to see so many communist activities around the campus. Most of the groups were professional students, a little older than the average student. They gave parties, passed out reading material, and had what was called Head Sessions. Everyone sat around and talked about politics.

The main topic was the federal government's illegal persecution of American citizens and socialist heroes. Some of the favorite subjects were Leon Trotsky and Arthur Miller. In the late fifties, Miller was a hero to non-conformist around the world. His Contempt of Congress conviction for failing to give names to the Committee mobilized the movement temporarily but had turned Hollywood into a paranoid community.

It became an international headline, but the biggest story in the newspapers was at the trial. One of the Congressional Committee members said he would vote to drop the case if Marilyn would pose in a picture with him. Arthur Miller said no thanks. I did not see a comment by Marilyn on this.

I had seen television accounts and news clips, which showed Marilyn at his side at various court appearances. After the Court of Appeals had overturned Miller's conviction, he was agitated that as a condition of the dismissal, the Committee urged him to write something less tragic about America.

Government officials encouraged Miller to begin work on "*The Misfits*," which was to star Marilyn and an aging American box office icon named Clark Gable.

After many heated conversations between Marilyn and Miller, concerning the screenplay, shooting commenced on *The Misfits*. She had envisioned it as containing a serious dramatic role for her without the sexual implications. She knew the language of the House Committee and the type of portrayal she desired.

The production did not go smoothly, and it became her last completed film. Directed by John Huston and co-starring Clark Gable, Montgomery Clift, and Eli Wallach, *The Misfits*, opened to mixed reviews. During the filming, the press reported public arguments about the dialogue between the Strasbergs and Miller.

As I continued to scribble down points of interest, an intriguing name began to appear on the pages, Psychiatrist Dr. Ralph Greenson. He was one of the doctors who had reported Marilyn's death.

She wrote:

"Frank introduced me to Doctor Greenson. He was able to get me some pills that relaxed

me. I wondered if Frank knew Greenson was a party member."

Later she wrote:

"Dr. Greenson spent hours with me discussing world politics. It reminded me about some of the talks I had with Arthur."

Doctor Ralph Greenson would play a significant role in the events that would transpire during the final year of Marilyn's life. No foreign policy issue was more sensitive than Cuba and its Russian allies in the early sixties. Anything Marilyn passed on to Dr. Greenson concerning what the Kennedy's said privately would have breached National Security.

There wasn't nearly enough time to read all that was in this journal, yet I continued thumbing through the diary looking for leads. Marilyn had written so much. The notes I was taking were just snapshots of the stories she was describing—something to help me remember what she had written. Familiar names and organizations equally caught my attention.

The next entry I read was about her relationship with the President of the United States, John F. Kennedy.

Marilyn wrote:

"The best day of my life. I met Jack at Peter's house. He was introduced as Senator John Kennedy and the next president of the United States. I wanted to stay calm, but he

was so exciting. His confidence, intelligence, and charm struck me. It lit a fire. We started seeing each other."

Her reference to Jack kind of threw me, but this was John Kennedy's nickname. Over the next few pages, it was apparent that Marilyn became involved with John Kennedy. There were graphic accounts of their relationship as she recalled "Kinky" parties they attended. Marilyn seemed to enjoy that lifestyle. Although she was still married to Arthur Miller at this time, according to her notes, she was continually in the company of John Kennedy.

She penned all of these entries:

"The thing with Jack was getting hot. I love all that real-life drama. Just think I'm in on it."

"Got to see Jack every time he came to New York City. I was close to Arthur and working regularly too."

"I was with the next President, and we made violent love."

She drew a couple of cartoons after that entry. The biggest one was a happy face.

After John Kennedy's election to President, Marilyn divorced Miller and soon after began in earnest the last phase of her life. Marilyn started attending meetings in New York with JFK and members of the Central Intelligence Agency. She referred to them as the "Spy

Boys." It wasn't clear if she was taking part in these discussions or just window dressing.

She wrote this about one of the meetings:

"The spy boys were really serious about killing Castro. Big Jim and a guy named Eduardo were actually involved in the Bay of Pigs. Jack never let them forget it."

The Bay of Pigs had been a big CIA disaster in Cuba during the early months of Kennedy's administration. With the US Government's support, a CIA-trained force attempted to invade southern Cuba to overthrow Fidel Castro. The invasion was launched in April 1961, less than three months after John F. Kennedy assumed the presidency. The Cuban armed forces easily defeated the invading combatants within three days.

It was quite interesting to see Marilyn writing about the Bay of Pigs. That incident was a very intense time for many Americans. However, decades would pass before I would discover the identity of the two men she mentioned in that entry. The Big Jim she was talking about was Jim O'Connell, a CIA operative documented as being in charge of the Agency's Castro Assassination plot.

O'Connell and President Kennedy were meeting to adopt the plan to assassinate Fidel Castro with Marilyn looking on. Eduardo, who she had mentioned, was none other than Howard Hunt of Watergate fame. Hunt was the head of Kennedy's covert operations in Cuba. It appears these meetings were formulating the highest level of information gathering and clandestine activities.

While reading Marilyn's diary, I made notes of three separate meetings she attended with Central Intelligence Agents. In recent years, Congressional disclosures have verified her accounts of these conversations. At some meetings, she noted that Mafia high rollers, Sam Giancana and Johnny Roselli, were also in attendance. Her writings disclosed that Roselli discussed a previous attempt to assassinate Castro.

She said of that meeting:

We attended a meeting with the spy boys and mafia gangsters. They were discussing how to kill Castro. Johnny Roselli boasted about the Mafia's ability to infiltrate anybody's security to kill them. They had a pill to cram up Castro's butt."

Later CIA documents quoted Roselli, saying a Cuban with Mafia ties tried to mix the pill in Castro's drink but got cold feet. He also said the CIA provided a suppository for insertion into a person's rectum. Were these tools of the trade a clue to Marilyn's killing?

I could never tell if she interacted with all these officials or their underworld associates. She wrote what she thought about the meetings and conversations, but didn't give a clue regarding her participation. One thing was sure; Marilyn was involved not only with the White House, FBI, and CIA but some of the most dangerous gangsters of that time.

With knowledge of secret American attempts to overthrow at least two foreign governments and the President's association with Mafia figures, Marilyn found herself right in the middle of world politics. I couldn't help but think to myself, "So have I."

Regardless of everything, it was apparent that part of Marilyn enjoyed the intrigue and interaction that came with the CIA. They had begun to take up a great deal of her time, which showed in her writings. Her topics changed from killing Castro to other clandestine activities.

She made these entries about her activities with the CIA:

"Big Jim wanted me to do a job for them. They were trying to bring down a foreign leader, who doesn't want to cooperate."

"Bob and Big Jim talked about shooting a film with Howard Hughes to embarrass this diplomat."

"Bob said we were going to see Mr. Hughes to set it up."

It took a little time for these pages to make sense to me, but I knew Howard Hughes was one of the richest men in the world. What I didn't realize was that Hughes was also the government's largest contractor.

Hughes had introduced one of Hollywood's more controversial films when he released "The Outlaw." The production featured one of Marilyn's friends, Jane

Russell, who defied the set standard of morally acceptable content in motion pictures by showcasing her breasts. Terry Moore, another one of Marilyn's friends, had also been married to Hughes.

Hughes and Robert Maheu formed a partnership that participated in CIA activities regularly. The foreign leader in question was Indonesian President Achmad Sukarno, deemed to be communist influenced by the CIA.

Big Jim O'Connell had received a promotion to Chief of Far East Operations. He remembered Marilyn and knew she could assist him with this high-level assignment.

Marilyn wrote:

"They set up photo ops at a couple of hotels, and when the diplomat came to visit Jack, he was seen with me."

Marilyn had also spent some time in Mexico. She wrote about a meeting with the Fair Play for Cuba Committee.

"At the meeting, I heard the Cubans were being pushed into the Soviet Bloc by American policy. They love Castro. I don't think Big Jim will ever get him."

Later, I found out the senior FBI official in Mexico had taken notice and sent Director J. Edgar Hoover, a four-page report. It said that Monroe had associated closely with individual members of the American

Communist Group and visited the Cuban and Soviet Union Embassies.

The CIA identified one of the people she associated with as a person of interest in a Cuban missile deployment file. FBI disclosures deleted his name. One of this man's companions at the Cuban and Soviet Embassies would later waltz into the history books, Lee Harvey Oswald.

Marilyn never mentioned either man's name in the book, but the possibility exists of them crossing paths. I can't imagine a steady trail of American tourists with CIA ties visiting these embassies. However, this common denominator of English speaking people in a Spanish speaking country would be enough for a chance meeting.

FBI Director Hoover labeled Marilyn a national security risk. Many have speculated on why she was in Mexico City. Perhaps this memo helped cover-up what her real motives were. Whatever information Marilyn gathered while she was at the Embassy's or in private conversations has never been disclosed. Still, I'm sure the data is in some file maintained by a federal agency.

The diary might have had more information, but there was not enough time to read the details more thoroughly. This trip did appear to be much more than it seemed, and as the years passed, I came to believe that it might have gravely impacted Marilyn's life and death.

In 1962, I had no real idea about what this diary meant. Still, it was easy to understand how documenting these events could pose a problem. Marilyn was involved not only with the White House and Organized Crime, but the CIA's overthrow of foreign governments. After her trip to Mexico City, the FBI also considered her a security risk.

J. Edgar Hoover was concerned about Marilyn's relationship with the Kennedy's. In a memo released under the Freedom of Information Act, he discussed a meeting and conversation on world politics Marilyn had with John Kennedy at actor Peter Lawford's house. How could he have known what they discussed? Did Hoover have Lawford's house tapped?

I began to realize that her public perception as a dumb blond in her films and her sex goddess image seemed superficial compared to this well written expose'. It told the story of a seemingly complicated existence. Marilyn found herself thrust into an environment that she had no control over. I believe she had gotten in deeper than anybody ever realized, and according to her writings, things began to unravel.

She stated:

"My life is very confusing after Jack became President. I want to go to the White House all dressed up like when I met the Queen, but I'm not his damn wife. That's so depressing."

In 1962, as news of her affair with the President became a discussion in Washington, her now-famous appearance in New York seemingly was the straw that broke the camel's back.

"Peter asked me to sing Happy Birthday during Jack's party at Madison Square Garden. I finally met his brother Bobby. It was fun but didn't work out."

Although her "Happy Birthday Mr. President" performance made big headlines, it was not a particularly good night for Marilyn. The First Lady, Jackie Kennedy, was there along with the rest of the family. Years later, I spoke with Marilyn's friend, Jeanne Carmine, who told me that someone had threatened Marilyn not to show up that night. Jackie was aware of her affair with JFK and had confronted him about it.

However, the most intriguing part about the entry was Marilyn mentioning meeting Bobby Kennedy for the first time. Bobby was the Attorney General then, and I was very familiar with him. About a year earlier, he had delivered a powerful radio broadcast for Voice of America, defending America's record on race relations to the rest of the world.

When I first heard him give that address, I remember thinking how idealistic he sounded. Bobby Kennedy had a passion and struck me as someone who cared about the struggles of Black people.

During that time, the Freedom Riders were the talk of the African-American community. Both Kennedy brothers had taken that opportunity to begin building a rapport with civil rights leaders. Many initiatives that occurred during the Kennedy Administration were a result of the passion and determination of Robert

Kennedy. He underwent a thorough conversion of purpose as their relationship expanded.

In September 1961, Bobby Kennedy requested the Interstate Commerce Commission to make rules banning all segregated seating in interstate terminals and vehicles.

This ruling gave the Freedom Riders an unequivocal victory in their campaign. Students from all over the country purchased bus tickets to the South and crowded into jails in Jackson, Mississippi. With the participation of northern students, even more, press coverage transpired. As more people in the U.S. learned about the Freedom Riders, more wanted to support them.

The country felt sorry about the unnecessary violence and lack of police protection for the Freedom Riders, which embarrassed the United States on the world stage.

Seeing Bobby's name in Marilyn's writings was as surprising as anything I had seen up to this point. Never could I have imagined what his role would be in this case and subsequent cover-up.

As I continued flipping through the pages, I began to notice something else. It was starting to become more challenging to ascertain whether Marilyn was writing about past or current events. One thing was unquestionable; things had not been going well since the President's birthday party.

This very impassioned entry would follow:

"Jack stopped taking my calls. He even had the nerve to change his phone number. Peter told me Jackie was raising hell and would divorce him if he ever saw me again. Wish she had left him. I could have been his wife. I'm not afraid of these aristocrats."

The page was long, something she had not done since earlier parts of the book. Kennedy yielded to his wife's demand, and that's when Bobby's name began to appear frequently on the pages. Evidence suggests that John sent his brother to explain why he couldn't see her again. Now, if John lit a fire inside Marilyn, Bobby was like a nuclear explosion. According to her diary, she fell head over heels in love with him.

After that, her tone seemed to change. When she began writing again, it was a more serious Marilyn that emerged. It was as though she stopped looking back and was documenting the moments. There were notations of days and dates on some pages. Without a doubt, she was now keeping an account of her current activities.

I made note of a meeting she attended with Bobby Kennedy.

"Big meeting in San Diego. Jim was there, and Bobby was glad to see him. I love being with Bobby. He says we're going to make America the most powerful country in the world."

For ten pages or so, Bobby and Marilyn were acting like teenage lovers. The entries were steamy with conversations of love and marriage on almost every page.

The way she described it gave me the impression that this was a joyful time of her life.

Although the book was captivating, none of it offered any real assistance to finding a next of kin. Wanting a second opinion about the book, I walked over to Lester Goldberg's desk and asked him if we were still on for lunch. He told me to give him a minute, and then we went to grab a bite.

As we sat down to eat, Lester told me he had received some very high-level phone calls about Marilyn's case. He said,

"They're asking some pretty strange questions about our investigation, and it seems like they're looking for something. All of it is very unusual."

I pulled the book out and told him this had arrived with her property. Showing him some of the entries, Goldberg knew this book would be something of interest to the press and federal authorities. He said,

"This information could be used by anyone with a bone to pick with the Kennedy's. I'm glad it's your case because I don't want investigators asking me about this hot potato. Good luck finding what you need, but you better be careful. I'll let you know if I hear anything else."

When I got back from lunch, the paperwork from my workload was beginning to pile up. After making a few phone calls, I tried gathering some information for my other cases. Armand came to me with the preliminary toxicology report. This test would disclose what was in the blood, and they did not find much. There was no poison in the stomach, presenting the possibility she had not ingested any pills. We looked at each other, and then I asked him,

"Did you check with the medical department if this is true?

Armand nodded yes and said,

"Abernathy has sent out the samples for further microscopic examination. You better make out some kind of statement for the press."

The examination would take 4 to 6 weeks. We would need a medical determination before I could request Dr. Curphey to order a full police investigation, or at least a coroner's inquest.

Assigned to perform the autopsy was Dr. Thomas Noguchi, and he was the best the County had to offer. He was a no-nonsense kind of guy whose professionalism made our job a little easier when dealing with medical questions from the family. Having a doctor there made things contentious. He was the only one who would take the time to explain a cause of death to family members or the Coroner's representative, who was on the case. Most of the other Autopsy Surgeons did not want anything to do with the family, press, or the police.

I went to the autopsy room to see if there was anything he needed from our unit for the autopsy. When I arrived, Dr. Noguchi and Deputy District Attorney John Miner, were there talking. Miner was a liaison between the District Attorney's medical-legal section and the Coroner's office. He carried medical information, identification certifications, and personal property between our office and theirs. Miner visited us often, and we had worked together several times in the past. The fact that he was going to present at the autopsy showed the District Attorney's office had a particular interest in the case.

Marilyn's body was lying on the gurney, covered by a sheet and getting prepped for the autopsy. Miner and Noguchi were looking at some bruises on her leg. I could clearly see a bruise just below the knee. Dr. Noguchi explained that this was common because many people fall or the body gets bruised when being handled after death. I wasn't a doctor, but this didn't look like a bruise from a fall. Besides, wasn't she was found dead on a bed? My first thought was needle mark, but obviously, Dr. Noguchi didn't concur.

Something else was bothering me. Why was Deputy District Attorney Miner in the autopsy room a day before the autopsy? He had received authorization to witness Dr. Noguchi perform Marilyn's autopsy the following morning at 8:00 am. In a non-homicide investigation, this was extremely irregular.

Not wanting to disturb them, I told Dr. Noguchi to let me know if he needed anything for the autopsy. I decided to check back with Deputy Danbacker to see what he found at the house. Danbacker had been with the Coroner's office for a couple of years. He was an immigrant European and spoke with a very thick accent.

Nobody at the office could pronounce his first name, so we all called him Danbacker.

He told me that someone thoroughly cleaned the house, and there weren't any prescription containers or medication anywhere.

I asked him to tell me what he saw when he picked up the body the day before, hoping he could shed a little light on things.

The Deputy told me she was found dead in her bedroom, but it was easy to see someone moved the body because of the discoloration. He also reiterated that she had died much earlier because rigor mortis had already begun to set in. Upon completing the final physical diagram and the autopsy report, no mention of these details, or the bruise marks on her body, were reported.

I returned to my desk and just sat there a moment. My head was literally spinning from this investigation. Nothing was making any sense, and on top of everything else, there was that crazy diary. I looked at my pages of messy notes, which had no executor, no next of kin, or any indication of who should be responsible for her burial.

Time was running short. By then, I had already concluded there would be no executor listed in this book, but it no longer mattered. My investigation had taken a completely different turn. The more I tried to make sense of the strange circumstances surrounding her death, the more I realized something was very wrong.

First, somebody tries to remove the body from the house, now no poison is found in her stomach, yet everybody is still yelling suicide.

All I could do was keep reading. Marilyn began describing detailed accounts of her encounters with Bobby Kennedy. She wrote about his fierce courtroom battle with Jimmy Hoffa, which was covered intensely by the media.

She wrote:

"Bobby was on the phone most of the night talking to Jack. It was something about putting that guy Hoffa in jail."

In recalling the writings, I never had the feeling that she was a frantic woman, and her descriptions seemed well thought out. It was plain to see why she was consciously writing it down. She was subconsciously trying to process the information.

But things began to change. Marilyn wanted more from her relationship with Bobby Kennedy. According to Jeanne Carmine, she heard Marilyn on the phone at her house, telling him to leave his wife on more than one occasion. But he was Catholic, and a divorce would surely destroy his political career.

She jotted:

"I asked Bobby again about us. He told me, don't be ridiculous. Said he was going to become President after Jack, and I'm not going to ruin it."

For the first time, I began to see a sense of desperation on the pages. In the beginning, Marilyn described almost everything in detail, sometimes taking 2 or 3 pages. Now everything was short and to the point. On one particular page, she portrayed another interaction with Kennedy.

Someone had told him that she was keeping notes on their activities. Bobby confronted Marilyn about the book.

"Bobby found out about my diary. Can't believe he raised holy hell for writing about us. Told me to destroy it. Never thought he would react like that."

Marilyn's dream of a future with Bobby Kennedy began falling apart. Her passages became shorter and angrier as she began to realize the truth of her situation.

"Couldn't reach Bobby, and he won't call back."

"The dirty bastard changed his number. He thinks he going to do me like his brother did. I'll fix them all."

I put the diary back down and grabbed the press release on my desk. Marilyn had scheduled a press conference that Tuesday, according to the press release in her purse. Topic: "Marilyn Reveals it All."

Was this book what she had planned to disclose? Although my understanding of what Marilyn was saying wasn't clear, I knew that if she talked to the press about what she had written, the country was in for a shock.

It was around three o'clock by then, and some other cases still needed closing out before going home. I picked up the diary and thumbed down towards the end of the book.

Marilyn's desperation became even more evident. She seemed to have much more of an 'I don't care' attitude, and her next several entries reflected that feeling.

She wrote:

"Frank called tonight, maybe I'll go to Tahoe and let my hair down."

On the final weekend in July, Marilyn flew to Lake Tahoe, Nevada, for an exclusive Frank Sinatra party. According to her accounts, she met Teamster Leader Jimmy Hoffa, who was there with Mafia boss Sam Giancana.

She penned:

"I met Jimmy Hoffa at Frank's party. Made a big fool of myself. Drank too much and smoked too much. Sam and him were asking about Bobby. What did I say?"

The next couple of pages were intense, as Marilyn struggled to cope with her and Bobby's relationship. In some cases, her writings were incoherent, as if she were drunk or using drugs.

She wrote about a phone call.

"Peter called. Bobby is coming tomorrow. They want me to call off the press conference. Too late."

Peter Lawford and Bobby Kennedy knew about the press conference. But what did that prove? Would they have killed her for that? I kept reading. She went on to describe the first of two hostile visits by Kennedy.

"Bobby was really mad. Acted crazy and searched all my stuff. Told him it's mine. I'll never let him have it."

That was the last coherent entry Marilyn made in her diary. There was no doubt her later accounts were more relevant to her death. I flipped through the final pages glancing at the writing. It seemed as though she had become detached, and the entries weren't legible. There was obviously something wrong.

I didn't know what to make of what I had just read. Bobby Kennedy had an altercation with Marilyn over this diary. There was no date on this entry, so it was difficult to establish the time between when she wrote this and when she died. But I had to ask myself, was this the final night?

There were more questions than answers about this journal, diary, or whatever it was. I decided to turn the book over to Dr. Curphey, but he was already gone. Thinking Lester may have discovered something new, I walked over to see him, he had left as well. After spending the entire day dealing with this case, talking to investigators, gathering paperwork, answering phone calls, and reading the diary, I just wanted to put everything away and go home.

Dr. Noguchi had scheduled the autopsy for the next morning. So I straightened out my desk, took the diary, and locked it in the safe with the rest of her property. With Tuesday and Wednesday off, a short vacation from the Coroner's Office sounded like just what the doctor ordered. The preliminary autopsy report would be ready when I got back, and that was going to tell a big part of the story. I grabbed my notes and left. I needed to wrap my head around the events of the past two days.

CHAPTER 5:
The Cover-Up

Visions of the Kennedys, FBI, CIA, Castro, and Jimmy Hoffa were dancing around in my head as I drove home. Marilyn Monroe had been working for the Federal Bureau of Investigation and Central Intelligence Agency. These were two of the most powerful organizations in the world. The CIA, who most Americans knew little about during that time, was formed when Congress passed the National Security Act in 1947. It replaced the Office of Strategic Services as America's spy agency and intelligence-gathering group.

Although America's elected officials funded the agency, the general public didn't know or want to know what they were doing. I knew nothing about the Central Intelligence Agency but was a fan of CBS Network News. That kept me reasonably informed for political conversations around the office. But these subjects are not what I talked about with my friends.

Television broadcasts and major market newspapers were the only sources of national news. The only way you could find out about this secretive group was to have someone write about them or a television newscast. As I found out later, journalism was a perfect cover for CIA agents. People talk freely to journalists, and few thought suspiciously of a journalist aggressively asking questions or searching for information.

Not surprisingly, the CIA had begun a mission to recruit American journalists on a wide scale. They wanted these journalists to relay any sensitive information they had discovered and write anti-communist, pro-capitalist, and pro-CIA propaganda when needed. In the 1950s, the CIA contracted and paid some 3,000 people to further its policies. They would use many of them for this cover-up.

On the other hand, their counterparts, the Federal Bureau Of Investigation, and its Director, J. Edgar Hoover, had a broad reputation for dealing with crime and communism. Films and television shows were presenting them as being all that was good in America.

Some of the harshest criticism of Hoover, and the FBI, was spying on elected officials. Their Counter Intelligence Program, also known as COINTELPRO, was notorious for disrupting the Communist Party, and later, organizations such as the Black Panther Party and Martin Luther King Jr.'s Southern Christian Leadership Conference.

Their methods included infiltration, burglaries, illegal wiretaps, planting forged documents, and spreading false rumors about key members of target organizations. Trying to understand Marilyn's involvement in all this was nearly impossible. As I crept along through the Monday evening traffic, I was just glad the day was over.

It always felt good coming home to the sanity of my family. Along with my wife and three kids, we lived at a house in Pacoima, 15 miles north of downtown Los Angeles. It was an integrated working-class neighborhood where everybody knew each other.

My wife was overwhelmed by the depth of Marilyn's writings after glancing through the names and far-reaching details of the notes. When I told her how the press would love to have this information, she advised me to throw my notes away.

Her mother, who worked as a stenographer for the Los Angeles Police Department, agreed. I remember what she told me,

"Your family is the number 1 priority. You've got a job most colored men would love to have. Why would you slander the Kennedy's when it looks like they are going to do something good for this country? The Police Department will handle it."

I never liked being called a Colored, but I understood what they were saying. Besides, it was never my intention to let anyone else see my notes. My mother-in-law and her sister were dedicated civil service employees. They were trailblazers in City and County Government, active in local politics, and worked on various Ad-Hoc political Committees. I asked my mother-in-law what she thought about J. Edgar Hoover, and she said,

"The FBI is our last line of defense if we want law and order, especially now that we want civil and voting rights. They are doing what has to be done".

Her son and her sister's husband were both Teamsters, with whom I had many conversations about Jimmy Hoffa. I asked them that evening what did they know about the Hoffa-Kennedy feud. They contended that Kennedy represented the super-rich, and had it in for the Union, even though they had voted in high numbers for his brother. Both of them were giving total support to Hoffa against anybody.

I regularly had breakfast with them at some of the truck driver eateries in downtown Los Angeles. One of our favorite spots was the Original Pantry on 9th and Figueroa. On any given weekday morning, you could get a big slice of Americana just by dropping in. If there were any doubts about these unions' solidarity, you would quickly dismiss it once you were around them.

Their main concern was job security and wages for their families. The auto and aircraft workers were also in total support of their union's efforts. They represented the emerging middle-class environment taking the nation by storm, and their strength was at the ballot box.

Reading Marilyn's diary helped reshape my notion of reality, opening my eyes to a different aspect of our society. Her accounts of involvement with the White House and other influential government agencies provided me with new insight into our Nation's Foreign and Domestic Policy.

The people she wrote about were leading America's efforts in Nuclear Weapons proliferation, International plots in Indonesia and other key domestic issues. They included Communism, Civil Rights, Labor, and Employment. Marilyn's diary raised serious questions about how political figures and Government Agencies were attempting to shape people's lives globally. It forced me to do research and look at what Marilyn had written. Who were these people she wrote about? Were these things true? What did it all mean?

Things were a little eerie for the next few days with strange cars driving up and down the street slowly. People in the neighborhood began to notice. One of my neighbors walked out and approached a vehicle parked in front of her house. When she asked the two men sitting inside who they were looking for, they just drove off. In our neighborhood, strangers only meant the police or a repo man. I never knew who they were, but they weren't just door-to-door salesmen.

While mowing the lawn on Wednesday morning, I noticed two peculiar cars driving slowly down the street. They were four-door official-looking cars with nothing to indicate who they were. I looked at them, and they looked at me. With all this activity, everybody had the feeling something was wrong.

After we discussed it, one of my neighbors suggested we call the police. My wife was an excellent ambassador, and she kept the emotions down, although I knew what she was thinking. Neither of us was sure if this was about the diary, and we didn't say a word. It would have been embarrassing for our neighbors to know these people were possibly watching me.

That night, as my wife and I watched the evening news, we saw coverage of Marilyn's Funeral. Joe DiMaggio finally had agreed to handle her arrangements. As we both sat there, quietly looking at the service, somehow, I felt connected to Marilyn. My determination to learn the truth about her death became more robust than ever.

There were a lot of things on my mind when I came back to work. After two days off, my desk was a mess, and nobody even took the time to stack the new paperwork neatly. Everything was out of order like someone was looking for something every so often.

Besides the new cases assigned to me, there was a stack of inquiries about the status of Marilyn's case. The preliminary results of the autopsy had arrived, showing no trace of any medication she was taking. The tests showed her blood contained none of the drugs from the empty prescription containers brought from her house.

Dr. Noguchi had found 30 Nembutal tablets lodged in her throat. Dr. Abernathy had requested further microscopic examination because the first test was inconclusive.

Well, I immediately thought that destroyed the suicide angle. If she had attempted to take her life by filling her mouth with pills, she had failed. I called Noguchi to ask if this lab report would change the status of the case. He said no because they were ordering additional tests on the tissues and the liver.

There was still no preliminary police report. Deputy Goldberg came over to my desk and said he had something for me. He stated,

"An Associated Press reporter told him that Robert Kennedy is somehow involved in this. His sources are saying that he was in the house the night she died."

Lester stood there, looking me directly in my eyes and said,

"Lionel, be careful because there is a gathering of eagles hovering over this particular case. LAPD and the FBI are crawling all over the city looking for some important evidence. Cover your butt."

Lester was always saying things like that, but there was something much more serious about this. He looked nervous, even scared, and that wasn't like him. Those words, however, turned out to be prophetic. The eagles did begin to circle over my head, and I didn't have my hat on.

Dr. Curphey had issued a statement that he wanted all information about the Monroe case, coming in or going out, cleared with him. I decided there was no choice but to inform him about the diary. I went to retrieve it from the safe and discovered someone had removed it. I grabbed the sign-out sheet to see who took it, but there was no record of the book's removal. It wasn't only her diary. Everything had disappeared.

I reported the missing property to Phil Schwartzberg, my supervising deputy, and Richard Rathbun, my department head. Rathbun was a forty-year county employee who followed Dr. Curphey's instructions to the letter. He was one of only three people who had his own office within the Coroner's department and had keys to every vital lock. When I informed them about her property, they seemed unconcerned and told me the contents would turn up.

Their response was surprising to me because of Dr. Curphey's explicit orders regarding evidence in this case. However, there was nothing I could do or say about it, so I simply went on with my other duties. Maybe they knew what had happened to it and didn't want to tell me, but there was no way of knowing. I couldn't help but ask myself how many other people found out about the book while I had been away from the office?

After returning to my desk, Armand came over. He said Marilyn's press agent, Pat Newcomb, had come into the office, while I was off and asked about Marilyn's property. Armand said he looked in the safe, but nothing was there, and the log sheet said nothing. He mentioned that he spoke to Lester, who told him I had it on Monday. Amazed at his timing, I told him her property was missing, and my thoughts were that Dr. Curphey probably had it.

After I thought about it, Deputy Danbacker and Deputy Goldberg were the only ones who knew about Marilyn's articles being at the Coroner's Office. There was no reason for anybody else to be looking through her property unless they were looking for something specific.

Since her property was not signed out, it was logical to assume Dr. Curphey had it in his possession. One thing was for sure; whoever took her property out of the safe would have seen the explosive nature of Marilyn's diary. By now, some government agency or police department official may have looked at it. The White House certainly would have had an interest, and I know the Secret Service was looking around that Sunday morning. There was also a flip side. What if it got into the wrong hands? There could be far-reaching ramifications.

Although Marilyn's funeral had occurred the day before, her body remained the Los Angeles County Coroner's property. The Public Administrator, Baldo Kristovich, had allowed the release of her body for the funeral service. However, its return to the morgue was necessary, until a next of kin ruling. The final part of this investigation was gathering all medical data, including toxicology reports and autopsy results, along with the additional police information needed to close this complicated case.

The public was wondering why Marilyn was still in the County morgue. They called over 200 times a day with questions about her death. True to his word, Dr. Curphey had assigned the infamous Suicide Investigation Team to research the evidence. He appointed Dr. Robert Littman, a psychiatrist, and Dr. Norman Farberow, a psychologist, to probe the case. They were a pair of doctors from a Los Angeles Suicide Prevention Organization commissioned to find out everything about Marilyn's personal life. After concluding an investigation, they would submit an official report stating, in their professional opinion, whether she was a likely candidate for suicide.

My supervisor, Deputy Schwartzberg, asked me to work with the team that morning to arrange a press conference. Dr. Curphey wanted to assure the country that the team would interview, under oath, everyone who could shed light on her death. He said the press release should include a statement guaranteeing a thorough Coroner's investigation, utilizing their subpoena power for witnesses, and calling for an inquest if necessary.

Schwartzberg told me the Los Angeles Police Department was under extreme pressure from Washington to close their case, and we were too. He said we shouldn't expect LAPD to provide further reports on the circumstances and proceed without them.

He was faithful to what he said. Over the next week, I must have called 20 or so times to access a police investigation report, without success. However, something else strange had happened. Rumors circulated the office that someone from the D.A.'s office didn't believe Marilyn had committed suicide.

Trying to get more information, I went to see what Lester Goldberg knew. He told me that Deputy District Attorney John Miner had sent a memo to Dr. Curphey about the autopsy and an interview he did with Dr. Ralph Greenson. Miner said Greenson told him Marilyn wasn't suicidal. Lester said, "Curphey's not budging."

That same day, they told me to arrange another press conference, announcing the Suicide Investigation Team's findings. It was difficult to believe these doctors could complete their analysis so quickly, but I scheduled the press conference.

On August 17, 1962, Dr. Curphey made this statement to press members from around the world:

Statement by Theodore J. Curphey, M.D.
Chief Medical Examiner-Coroner
County of Los Angeles

Now that the final toxicological report and that of the psychiatric consultants have been received and considered, it is my conclusion that the death of Marilyn Monroe was caused by a self-administered overdose of sedative drugs and that the mode of death is probable suicide. The final toxicological report reveals that the barbiturate, previously reported as a lethal dose, has been positively identified as Nembutal by the toxicologist. In the course of completing his routine examination, the toxicologist Dr. Raymond Abernathy discovered in addition to the Nembutal present a large dose of chloral hydrate.

Following is the summary report by the Psychiatric Investigative Team, which has assisted me in collecting information in this case. This team was headed by Robert Litman, M.D., Norman Farberow, Ph. D., and Norman Tabachnick, M.D.:

Marilyn Monroe died on the night of August 4 or the early morning of August 5, 1962. Examination by the toxicology laboratory indicates that death was due to a self-administered overdose of sedative drugs. We have been asked, as consultants, to examine the life situation of the deceased and to give an opinion regarding the intent of Miss Monroe when she ingested the sedative drugs, which caused her death. From the data obtained, the following points are the most important and relevant:

Miss Monroe had suffered from psychiatric disturbance for a long time. She experienced severe fears and frequent depressions. Mood changes were abrupt and unpredictable. Among symptoms of disorganization, sleep disturbance was prominent, for which she had been taking sedative drugs for many years. She was thus familiar with and experienced in the use of sedative drugs and well aware of their dangers.

Recently one of the main objectives of her psychiatric treatment had been the reduction of her intake drugs. This has been partially successful during the last two months. She was reported to be following doctor's orders in her use of the drugs; and the amount of drugs found in her home at the time of her death was not unusual.

In our investigation, we have learned that Miss Monroe had often expressed wishes to give up, to withdraw, and even to die. On more than one occasion in the past, when disappointed and depressed, she made a suicide attempt using sedative drugs. On those occasions, she had called for help and had been rescued.

From the information collected about the events of the evening of August 4th, it is our opinion that the same pattern was repeated except for the rescue. It has been our practice with similar information collected in other cases in the past to recommend a certification for such deaths as probable suicide.

Additional clues for suicide provided by the physical evidence are: (1) the high level of barbiturates and chloral hydrate in the blood which, with other evidence from the autopsy indicates the probable ingestion of a large amount of the drugs within a short period of time; (2) the completely empty bottle of Nembutal, the prescription for which was filled the day before the ingestion of the drugs; and (3) the locked door which was unusual.

On the basis of all the information obtained, it is our opinion that the case is a probable suicide.

The Suicide Investigation Team had determined that Marilyn Monroe had suffered from depression and severe mood changes for many years. That, combined with an alleged history of substance abuse, led them to believe she probably took her own life.

Laws did not require these doctors to reveal their sources of information. However, according to their statement, most of their conclusions were based on psychological evaluations performed while Marilyn was still alive. There was only one person in Marilyn's life performing these evaluations: her psychiatrist, Dr. Ralph Greenson.

The same Associated Press reporter who spoke with Lester Goldberg grilled Littman and Farberow during the question and answer session. He asked about any evidence suggesting Marilyn Monroe could be a murder victim. They asked about rumors of Dr. Greenson recanting his statements regarding her being suicidal, and the presence of Robert Kennedy at her house the night she died. Both doctors calmly stated that those aspects of the investigation were outside their mandate and referred those questions to Los Angeles Police Department officials.

Dr. Littman also discussed reading published news accounts about her life. One such report mentioned was Marilyn's alleged nervous breakdown during her filming of the "Misfits" in 1960. Monroe left the movie set for ten days and supposedly checked herself into a hospital during that time. However, according to her diary, Marilyn was with John Kennedy at a Beverly Hills Fundraiser for his election campaign, describing the nervous breakdown as an excuse for a weeklong fling.

The Suicide Investigation Team also claimed they uncovered evidence showing Marilyn had tried to take her own life several times before. This information was undoubtedly also acquired from tabloid newspaper accounts. During my subsequent investigation of her case, I spoke with many of Marilyn's friends. None of her close acquaintances remembered when any actual suicide attempts ever occurred.

Dr. Littman and Dr. Farberow's report seemed to indicate that the Los Angeles Police Department had also guided and influenced their decision. That meant either they or Dr. Curphey had talked to police officials. After the press conference, I went to Dr. Curphey to obtain all data from the Suicide Team's investigation for Marilyn's private folder, and the people they interviewed for Marilyn's folder. Curphey informed me that these reports were all oral, and there are no written records available.

Because I was there, let me say that the Suicide Team never performed a thorough investigation. They provided me with a list of people they wanted to interview. Only three witnesses were set-up: Dr. Engelberg, Dr. Greenson, and Marilyn's publicist Pat Newcomb. I never could verify they spoke with these three, but no official record of any interviews exists. I even checked with the medical and investigative stenographers to ask about any notes submitted to them for typing. They all said no.

On the other hand, the police reports were public record, and copies accompanied each public file as a matter of course. The Los Angeles Police Department never sent a follow-up report, or Dr. Curphey must have personally received them. Either way, according to county ordinances, you couldn't close a case without these documents. I even asked Curphey if the Suicide team had received a police report. He said none of their information was available. Apparently, it was just a doctor's thing where they all sat around with Engelberg and Greenson to discuss and determine how she died.

In the days that followed, while gathering my files, all the original paperwork began to disappear. For instance, the original toxicology report showing no poison in the blood now revealed a high concentration of barbiturates in the liver. The new dosage in Marilyn's blood, which was determined before the microscopic test had returned, was enough to have killed her ten times over. The physical diagram that had shown the bruises on the body was gone and replaced by one that showed no marks. The original toxicology report was missing, and the police statement to our first call deputy was gone. Even the property log came up missing.

A few days later, while sitting at my desk, I was approached by a man claiming to be a forensics investigator from the office. I wasn't sure if I had seen him around before, but he said he needed to discuss some official business and asked could we meet for lunch. He seemed to know me on a first-name basis, but to this day, I am unable to recall his.

At lunch, he said that the higher-ups were concerned about my misgivings regarding the Monroe case. He asked me if I thought Marilyn's death was murder. I told him there wasn't enough evidence to support murder, but more than likely, she didn't commit suicide.

The man asked if I knew what happened to her property. I told him someone with a key removed it from the safe, without signing. His reaction seemed to suggest he thought I knew more, or perhaps even had it myself, but he didn't ask anything else about it. We ate lunch and talked for nearly an hour about the case and people at the office, including Dr. Curphey. He knew everybody by name and appeared to be genuinely concerned about me.

During our conversation, he steadily emphasized how important it was to be teammates and look out for each other. He said,

"Lionel, we all know you're a hard-working family man with three kids, and we're going to look out for you. As we were leaving, he handed me a credit card and told me, "this is to help you and the family get a little further ahead. Buy some things you need, and I'll get the card later."

It seemed a little odd, but for a young 22-year-old man and sole supporter of his family, all I could think was why not? Especially after that long pep talk about looking out for each other and being teammates. After finishing my shift, I went to a local tire store, and purchased new tires for my car, worn out from my daily ride downtown.

When I arrived back at work the next day, Dr. Curphey announced he or his administrative assistant would be answering all inquiries about the Monroe case. They revealed to the press that the overdose had been self-administered, and the pills swallowed in one gulp. This official statement was final and released to almost every news agency in the world.

I had read Dr. Noguchi's preliminary autopsy report, and he never concluded how these barbiturates entered Marilyn's body. There was never any official statement of those facts or any mention of the 30 pills that Dr. Noguchi found lodged in her throat. There was no trace of any other prescription drugs she was known to be taking.

There were plenty of phone calls from her friends and fans. Many thought the suicide finding was a slur on Marilyn's character and demanded the Coroner convene an Inquest into her death. Others, including the media, suspected someone else had administered the overdose, perhaps by injection or suppository.

Most disturbing was the fate of specimens taken from Monroe's body during the autopsy. When Dr. Noguchi asked the lab to test Marilyn's tissue samples again, he learned Dr. Curphey ordered them destroyed.

As for the Coroner's Office, the investigation into the death of Marilyn Monroe had come to an end. The case was put on my desk with instructions to close as soon as possible. The death certificate inside the file identified the cause of death as acute barbiturate poisoning due to ingestion of overdose. In the space for Mode of Death, autopsy surgeon Dr. Thomas Noguchi circled Suicide, adding the word probable.

It was standard procedure that the Deputy who handles the investigation signs the death certificate on behave of the Coroner. His signature certifies the compliance of all laws for the State of California. I went to see Dr. Curphey for the necessary information to close the file. However, he told me he was not ready to release the information and sign it with what I had.

When asked about the inaccurate information in the file, Curphey went into a rage and said,

"Grandison, you are in over your head. I warned you about this. Sign it or else."

This was another incident of pressure from him to circumvent county policy. Normally, Curphey would have been adamant about following county rules and regulations, but it was apparent that Marilyn Monroe's case was anything but normal. He then handed me a press release stating:

PRESS RELEASE
There was no credible evidence supporting a murder theory. There was a possibility that the death had been accidental, but suicide was more likely.
Theodore Curphey, Coroner of Los Angeles County

He said to give all the Deputies this release and regard it as the official statement. I remember walking down the hall, saying to myself, "What business is this of mine? He's the boss, and if this is the way it's supposed to go, then so be it." He must have known something that wasn't part of the file. I thought maybe it's time for me to be a team player. So, reluctantly, I signed the death certificate and hoped never to hear the name Marilyn Monroe again.

Driving home, I remember having a bad taste in my mouth. Team player or not, everything about that Marilyn Monroe case was wrong, and now I was part of the cover-up. A few months earlier, I had seen another instance of Coroner's abuse of power. In April, LAPD had shot an unarmed Black Muslim at his house of worship. The Mayor of Los Angeles, Sam Yorty, had come out and arduously stated to not look at this "militant group" as having a house of worship.

He went on to say that the police had reason to believe that guns were at the location, and plots to undermine the government existed within this group. Of course, there were neither guns nor plots, just an innocent dead citizen and a lot of wounded people.

Previously, my only interaction with Muslims had been with their newspaper, Muhammad Speaks. I would buy it from time to time and read what they said about African American heritage. They were an aggressive group on the streets of Los Angeles, promoting a change in America's treatment of African Americans. The

Nation of Islam was part of the new revolutionary movement, which included the Black Panthers, Southern Christian Leadership Conference, and others pushing their idea of Freedom, Justice, and Equality.

I had never considered myself a part of these movements. Still, certain events, such as the lynching of 14-year-old Emmitt Till in Mississippi, made me wonder about the future of African Americans. In the case of Emmitt Till, the group of Ku Klux Klan members who ruthlessly battered and hung this teenager were found innocent of all charges.

California was not a place where they had segregated facilities. The courts ostensibly followed the law in dealing with African Americans. Most of the people who lived here were civilized and could see an integrated America's bright future. However, racism was still present, particularly in law enforcement and employment.

The Coroner's Office scheduled an Inquest to determine if anyone was criminally responsible for the death of Ronald Stokes, an African-American killed in South Central Los Angeles. The Inquest deputy was Charles Langhauser, who controlled the proceedings on behalf of the Coroner.

LAPD provided all the witnesses, and no private citizens were allowed to testify. Standard procedure was to have the City, District Attorney, or outside counsels, submit questions that Langhauser would ask under oath to any witnesses called. He alone had subpoena powers.

It was my case, and I received a call from the Stokes family attorney regarding the Inquest. He was asking about the procedure for submitting questions to the police officers. Giving the call to the Inquest Deputy, standing at my desk, I heard him tell the attorney,

"Just bring your questions to the Inquest, and there would be no problem."

Having worked many Inquests, I knew that all questions needed submission to the Inquest deputy seventy-two hours in advance.

On the day of the Inquest, the press pool heard there would be an appearance from Malcolm X, the proclaimed Black Militant. Malcolm embodied the struggle for equal justice under the law, which was essentially the same cry of the Civil Rights Movement under Dr. Martin Luther King.

The Washington Post and the New York Times had covered Malcolm X's accusation of the New York Police Department mishandling African American prisoners while in their custody. This was his first major incident on the West Coast.

He spoke to groups all around the city and led an effort to prosecute the officers involved in the shooting. When Malcolm X walked into the Coroner's Office, a hush came over the room. There were four well-groomed men with him, who were also Muslims, standing at attention near the counter. The family's lawyer, whose name was Charles Brody, walked in with them.

Brody was one of the top black legal minds in Los Angeles. His resume was extensive, and he was also the first to hire a young Johnny Cochran. He leaned on the counter and asked the clerk where to deliver his questions. Armand then called the supervising deputy, who explained that questions were not allowed due to their late submission. The hall was full of newspapermen and Inquest witnesses, mostly Los Angeles Police Officers, listening carefully to what was happening.

Malcolm cried cover-up, and a brief scuffle occurred. To avoid calling Sheriff Deputies, I pulled the Nation of Islam members aside, telling Malcolm to give me five questions. I then placed them under Inquest Deputy Langhauser papers on the bench. Although only one got asked at the Inquest, there was no doubt who was responsible for putting that question there.

The shooting was found to be justifiable, and no one was held criminally responsible. Although this meant another trip to Curphey's office, it established ties with the Muslim community played a huge part in my future. They were very appreciative of my efforts to give them a voice in the proceeding.

It's important to understand that every case was significant to me. My feelings were that government offices should be colorblind and administer the law equally. I handled all kinds of cases, including sudden deaths for no reason, tragic accidents where identification was in question, homicides where life was ended in a cruel manner, and questionable and unquestionable suicides.

In most cases, the next of kin was devastated, and these were highly emotional times for the families. I signed temporary death certificates to get their loved ones buried, helped with legal matters such as insurance and estates. I also mediated next of kin problems that the investigating Deputy had to resolve. People who came into our office found a friend who would use the Coroner's Office's power to protect their rights when dealing with government agencies.

CHAPTER 6:
After The Coroner's Office

Despite still struggling with signing the death certificate, it was business as usual at the Coroner's office. There was never a shortage of work. However, things did seem a little less hectic with the stress of Marilyn's case behind me. That was very short-lived.

Days after closing the case, investigators from the District Attorneys office confronted me after arriving to work. They wanted to ask me some questions about a missing credit card. As it turned out, the card given to me by that man during lunch had come from the property of a closed Coroner's case. That credit card was still sitting at my desk, waiting for pick up. When I bought the tires using the credit card, it just didn't feel right, and I never used it again. After telling the investigators what happened and where the card was, I was arrested and taken to jail.

During my interrogation, an endless stream of police and law officials questioned me, but I never knew anybody. I tried to explain what happened, but my story must have seemed ridiculous. A guy, who said he was from the office, gave me the card and said, get myself some things? Even I had a hard time believing that story, and it had happened to me.

For years, I believed that Dr. Curphey had sent this man to set me up. Later, the possibility of a more massive conspiracy to discredit me became all too apparent.

Marilyn's diary contained highly sensitive information about United States Government agencies, and that book had been in my possession. Either way, it didn't matter. I had got caught in a huge bear trap, and there was no getting out.

The District Attorney asked me why someone would set me up like that. At the time, I really wasn't sure why this had happened, but what first came to mind was the Marilyn Monroe case and her diary. Lester Goldberg had told me this was a hot potato, and some heavy hitters were involved, but I never thought it could come to this.

There was no choice but to tell District Attorney investigators everything about the case and the existence of her diary. I described what she wrote about, including working for the FBI and her relationship with the Kennedy's. I explained how poorly our office handled her death investigation and how Dr. Curphey forced me to sign her death certificate.

After hours of interrogation, I was told not to mention this to anybody or talk about the man who originally stole the credit card. Complying with these terms would mean a lenient verdict. The District Attorney was not attempting to find the guy who had given me the stolen property. My attorney was livid when he discovered how candid my answers were. However, I didn't believe there was anything to hide. Unfortunately, in the end, I became the perfect fall guy.

Embarrassed and labeled a criminal, I resigned from the Coroner's Office in disgrace. The court ruled I hadn't stolen the card nor forged the name but was guilty of receiving stolen property and granted probation as my lenient sentence. The news media had a field day on the story.

As the dust began to settle, my next step was simply trying to get on with my life. With no income to pay the monthly rent and food bills, times quickly became difficult for our family. The prospects for employment were very slim because of my record and notoriety. After much soul-searching, I decided to enroll at Los Angeles City College and pursue a career in communications.

The world of television and radio had fascinated me since being a young child. At nine years old, I appeared on several episodes of the Art Linkletter "People Are Funny" television show. That experience captivated my imagination and influenced my interest in communications. I was fortunate to have a family that provided their full support. With me now taking classes, my wife began working for the first time, while my Grandmother helped with the kids.

A year later, I was stunned by the announcement of President John F. Kennedy's assassination. As I sat there watching the news report, all I could think about was Marilyn's diary. Could there have been a connection between what I had read and the President's death? I had a surreal feeling about the whole thing. It was like deja-vu. The only good thing was that I wasn't involved. Or was I?

As new information would begin to surface, I began to think the latter. Two days after Kennedy's death, a man killed his accused assassin, Lee Harvey Oswald, at Dallas Police Headquarters. That man, Jack Ruby, had extensive ties with Sam Giancana and the mafia.

The President's Commission on the Assassination of President Kennedy, better known as the Warren Commission, was established in the days following the Kennedy assassination. Reports began to surface that Lee Harvey Oswald had close ties to Cuba and the CIA.

Marilyn had written about the obsession President Kennedy and the CIA had with killing Castro. They were so desperate to kill him, that their plot included using Mafia gangsters.

The Warren Commission investigation uncovered some startling facts. The Russians and Cubans had considered Oswald a Federal Agent. The KGB suspected him of being a false defector, sent to Russia to spy for the United States. Castro claimed that when Oswald left Russia, he went to Mexico in search of information on the missile bases getting constructed off the coast of the United States.

Information about Oswald's stay in Mexico City before JFK's assassination was in a classified top-secret report. After receiving the report, the Warren Commission acknowledged the existence of CIA surveillance photos showing Oswald entering Fair Play For Cuba meetings in Mexico.

The disposition of these photographs and who else was in the photos did not get disclosed. There was no doubt Oswald was in Mexico in February 1962, leaving a strong possibility of him being there the same time as Marilyn. If I were to believe the Cuban scenario with the CIA and Mafia, or the other pages in her book, it didn't seem far-fetched to assume an Oswald-Marilyn connection.

These were the first pieces of a complicated puzzle that began to come together. Although I was an outsider looking in now, it was plain to see the same group of agencies was involved. There were still many more puzzle pieces and unanswered questions. However, two things were looming large in my mind. Who introduced Marilyn Monroe to John F. Kennedy, and why?

I went to work for a record distributor that marketed releases by Cameo Parkway artists Bobby Rydell and Chubby Checker. They were two of the biggest artists of the time. Just to show you the coincidence that has followed me, the first promotional campaign assigned to me, where my decisions really mattered, was a novelty remake of "Wild Thing" by an impressionist imitating Robert F. Kennedy under the name Senator Bobby. How dare this set of characters follow me into my private life.

Unfortunately, the death of John Kennedy brought back memories of Marilyn's case to someone other than me. It had been a very difficult time following my experience at the Coroner's Office—extremely tough on my wife and me. One evening, a few weeks following the assassination, she said,

"This whole situation is your fault. I told you to put that damn diary down and act like you never saw it. If you would have just did that and minded your own business, none of this would have ever happened."

The pressure had finally become too much for us. We agreed to separate and ultimately were divorced.

The time following my divorce was a difficult period of my life. Fortunately, I was still close to my kids, who were regular visitors at my Grandmother's house. My mother had moved in and was also babysitting. The love these two women provided during this time allowed me, and my ex-wife, to pursue our lives knowing our children always had someone willing and wanting to care for them.

During the mid-sixties, racial tensions in Los Angeles were at an all-time high. Black power movements such as the Nation of Islam, Black Panther Party, Student Non-Violent Coordinating Committee (SNCC), and other activists began confronting numerous issues facing the African-American community. Segregation, police brutality, and racism were something every black person in America had to deal with, and I was no different.

On February 25, 1965, the news of Malcolm X's killing stimulated something inside of me like never before. From the time we met in 1962 at the Coroner's office, and even before then, Malcolm represented the fighting spirit of all Americans who truly believed in the concept of freedom, justice, and equality. Rumors were floating around the black community, saying that the FBI was involved in Malcolm's death. When I thought about how the Federal Bureau of Investigation had used Marilyn Monroe back in the 1950s, it wasn't surprising to hear of their involvement. The rumors claimed that agents from the FBI had infiltrated the Nation of Islam and instigated the in-fighting between Malcolm and their leader, the Honorable Elijah Muhammad.

Years later, I would discover that both the CIA and FBI were making plans to assassinate Malcolm. A couple of names from the past came up, Robert Maheu and Johnny Roselli, both contracted to kill Malcolm, according to FBI disclosures. Marilyn wrote extensively about Maheu and Roselli in her diary. These two figures were still wreaking havoc in other people's lives. Another question also came to mind, did either of them have anything to do with Kennedy's assassination?

On August 12, 1965, a phone call from one of my associates, Earl Anthony, a law student from USC and Minister of Information for the Black Panther Party, awakened me. He said a California highway patrolman had arrested an entire family in Watts and roughed up the mother as a crowd of a couple of hundred people gathered around the scene.

There was a community meeting scheduled that afternoon, which Earl wanted me to attend. The purpose was to discuss solutions to the problems concerning public unrest in South Central Los Angeles. It was a little out of my area of expertise, but my friend felt there needed to be some young people involved. As I drove through the city, large crowds of people were gathered in the streets, throwing objects at cars, including police patrol ones.

The number one issue at the meeting was police brutality by the Los Angeles Police Department, with jobs and discrimination by the local business community a close second. About two hundred people gathered at the meeting, including preachers, church members, business owners, and a representative from the local Black bank. Many young African Americans, frustrated by the lack of employment opportunities, also attended. Labor unions were making their push with strikes across the country, and African Americans were making their stand against exclusion.

Low paying Civil Service jobs made up the bulk of workers in the African American community. Most of the income derived came from Los Angeles City or County employment because it was steady work. At that time, major corporations only hired 5% minority employees and divided that up between Latinos and Blacks.

The outcry that emerged against racism and discrimination exploded like a timebomb. Black leaders pleaded to restore order in the community, but it was too late. When I drove home, I heard a rallying cry from a local radio personality named Magnificent Montague, "burn, baby, burn". He was fond of yelling "Burn" when he played a hit record. When his listeners called him on the air, they followed suit. But this was no time for comedy, and the phrase set the tone for what was to come.

The Watts Riots began that night. By the time the second community meeting was convened, over 3,000 national guardsmen had joined the police, trying to maintain order on the streets. Jeeploads of heavily armed soldiers were prowling the neighborhoods and randomly shooting.

Inside a run-down, two-story building, across the street from Green Meadows Park in Los Angeles, several hundred angry citizens stated they didn't feel bad about what was happening. The general consensus was the time had come to make our feelings known, and police brutality was an excellent place to start.

"Burn, baby, burn," someone yelled, to a chorus of thundering applause.

I understood the anger and resentment the community was feeling towards the establishment. My life experiences had made me very sympathetic towards this type of violent reaction. However, I wasn't sure if this was the answer.

I once heard Malcolm X say how to avoid this type of civil disturbance.

"Step Up and Do For Self. We're paying taxes, and those tax dollars are what allows the police to beat us up. We have to develop our own economy to strengthen the black community."

Those remarks reflected my feelings towards our situation, and they needed to echo throughout South Central Los Angeles.

There was a curfew on, and the police were stopping cars to search for weapons. Officers were roughing up everybody, especially teenagers gathered in the streets. Leaving the meeting, I noticed members of the Black Muslim security team from Temple number 27 in Los Angeles. They were helping people who attended the meeting return safely to their cars and homes. One of them was Captain Edward Rasheed, who Malcolm X had introduced me to in 1962 at the Coroner's office incident.

Observing his professionalism and dedication to the community made me realize that every African-American had an obligation to their people. If rioting is not the answer, then we owe it to ourselves to discover what is. When the smoke cleared from the Watts Riots of 1965, 34 people had perished, over one thousand injured, and over thirty-five hundred American citizens arrested.

Marilyn's old friend, J. Edgar Hoover, linked the riots to Communist groups, who labeled unemployment and prejudice as the cause. LAPD Chief William Parker also fueled the tension by publicly labeling the people he saw involved in the riots as "monkeys in the zoo." In the end, one eye-catching fact was that before the Watts Riots, 69% of the Black community lived below the poverty level. This decreased to 39% in the years following, indicating the Black community's growth was alive and prospering.

In 1961, when Robert Kennedy headed the Justice Department, he promoted racial diversity in the formally all-white Justice Department. He appointed the largest number of African Americans to serve in any federal department up to that time. Kennedy strengthened the Civil Rights Division and stringently enforced laws protecting workers' right to organize trade unions and formally strike against employers.

He also began planning for a program called the 'War on Poverty." Marilyn and Bobby Kennedy were having their affair during that time. She described her meetings at the so-called Western White House with Kennedy and the other planners to one of her close friends. I did not read this in the diary, but during my conversation with her friend, Jeanne Carmen, she tried to put into context what Marilyn had said.

Marilyn told her, she convinced the War on Poverty planners that what was really needed was a new citizen's movement whose strength rested in grassroots community action. Carmine was astonished that Marilyn even knew anything about instruments for social change, but said Marilyn was very proud of herself.

The apparent result of these sessions was President Lyndon Johnson's War on Poverty. The strategy had begun in the Kennedy administration and provided Johnson with a format for the program. The Office of Economic Opportunity was fully committed to this grassroots strategy that Marilyn had suggested.

I had the opportunity to join this War on Poverty by attending classes at San Diego State University and the University of California, Berkeley. The Federal Government was recruiting candidates to operate their proposed manpower training programs. They were interviewing and testing throughout the country to get potential counselors and instructors to educate and prepare disadvantaged youth for the job market. The classes were held on at least six major university campuses and offered Masters Program credits for attending.

This brought together a highly motivated group of individuals who saw their role in society as preparing the minority community for its entrance into the majority culture. A small percentage of African Americans and Latinos received admission to this exclusive group. The administration soon realized how critical their perspective was for communicating with the minorities they were trying to train.

The Johnson Administration began to implement community action programs. These would provide training and employment for young men and women coming from impoverished families and neighborhoods.

They offered me a job as an employment specialist in this noble effort. The only problem was after we trained the disadvantaged youth, there were no jobs for them.

Disappointed with the program, I left Northern California and returned to Los Angeles, just in time, for the most unbelievable story of the year. Senator Robert Kennedy was assassinated—shot and killed in front of 50 or 60 eyewitnesses at the Coconut Grove Hotel in Los Angeles.

This Marilyn saga just refused to die. Now, all three of them were dead, and it was mind-bending. What were the odds of them all dying within less than six years of each other? They had to be astronomical. According to what I read in the diary, the relationship these three shared was extensive and intricate. Couldn't this really be a coincidence?

Both Kennedys were dead. Moreover, their murders were brutal. What did it all mean? During the past few years, I had been following how the JFK murder was quickly coming apart. New revelations had begun to surface about the CIA's involvement and accounts of multiple shooters.

There were 4 or 5 different accounts of Robert Kennedy's assassination. The person arrested, Sirhan Sirhan, was deemed psychotic by even prosecution psychiatrists and unfit to stand trial. But the judge disagreed, and Sirhan stood trial anyway. He would later claim he had been hypnotized or brainwashed. Sirhan was convicted and sentenced to death for assassinating Kennedy. The court later commuted his sentence to life.

My old friend, Dr. Thomas Noguchi, performed the autopsy. He said in the report that three bullets had hit Kennedy. A fourth damaged his suit coat and came upward at about an 80-degree angle. Noguchi and LAPD criminologist DeWayne Wolfer both conducted powder tests. They concluded that all three body shots came from about an inch away.

Later, Noguchi pointed out that he had refrained from saying whether there could have been a second shooter. The LAPD destroyed a large amount of evidence, and what survived from the police file was not released until twenty years later. What else was new?

This was a jigsaw puzzle of epic proportions. Two members of America's best-known family were dead, and one of Hollywood's most famous actresses was also. What did they all have in common? Marilyn's little red book. That was too much drama for me. I shook my head and said,

"This chapter of my life is now finally closed."

CHAPTER 7:
Marilyn Calls Out

In 1974, I was producing a Public Affairs radio series for Capital Cities Communications in Los Angeles. Cap Cities, as they came to be known, was a very progressive station group, who embraced Federal Communications Commission rules to provide programming for minority communities. In their major markets, WJR-AM-FM in Detroit and KPOL AM-FM in Los Angeles, they began broadcasting intelligent Public Affairs programs for Latino and African American audiences.

My organization, Project BAIT, was the producer of one of these shows. Spearheaded by Dave Rambo in Detroit, and my mentor Jim Crossen in Los Angeles, we were among the first to take advantage of these new FCC rules. We began airing a weekly show called "Who Cares," which became extremely popular and allowed me to meet various interesting people from many walks of life.

By chance, one of our producers scheduled an interview with an author who had written a book called "The Life and Curious Death of Marilyn Monroe." Now you can imagine my thoughts when that press release came to me. Twelve years after my hectic experience, Marilyn seemed to be calling out again.

The author's name was Robert Slatzer. I didn't know what to expect when he came into the studio. Slatzer's bio said he was the central voice that proclaimed Marilyn's death was not suicide. While our producer was interviewing him, I glanced through the pages of his book. His research was incredible. As I thumbed through, there was a chapter that discussed the autopsy and the Coroner's handling of the evidence.

Although he didn't have all the information right, he did have copies of original files from the case and numerous photos, including the crime scene. These were things I hadn't seen in more than a decade. While looking through the documents in his book, I discovered a copy of Marilyn's death certificate with my signature on it.

Listening to the interview, Slatzer had no doubt Marilyn's murder and the conspiracy to cover it up because of a Kennedy connection. His passion was striking. Slatzer said it was because he was once married to Marilyn, and Fox Studios had it annulled. I didn't know what to think about him, but the things he was saying began filling in some blanks like never before.

He told us a story about wire tapers who had bugged Marilyn's house. Bernard Spindel, an expert in audio surveillance and his partner Fred Otash, were hired by Teamster Union Boss Jimmy Hoffa to bug Marilyn's residence. Slatzer had uncovered massive details about these wire tapers and heard some of their recordings.

Slatzer said he discovered that Hoffa wanted to locate a diary that Marilyn had boasted was in her possession. The wire tapers claimed the union boss was desperately trying to blackmail Attorney General Bobby Kennedy. Hoffa wanted to make Kennedy drop the racketeering charges he was pursuing. They also informed Slatzer that the Giancana family in Chicago sent three members to keep an eye on the wiretap.

Mafia boss, Sam Giancana, knew that Marilyn had knowledge of his participation in the CIA plot to kill Castro. She had been present when he and Johnny Roselli agreed to participate in the scheme with President Kennedy and CIA operatives. The wire tapers said Giancana heard Marilyn tell some people about a press conference and her plans too, "Tell it All." They told Slatzer she had made these comments at a Frank Sinatra party in Lake Tahoe the weekend before she died.

Talk about a bombshell. Marilyn had written about that party in her diary and many other things, Robert Slatzer was corroborating. I was utterly stunned by what he was saying. How could this have happened? A man once married to Marilyn Monroe coming into the studio and confirming things I read in her diary. Yes, indeed, Marilyn was calling out.

When Slatzer finished the interview, I introduced myself and informed him of my connection to the case. The look on his face was priceless. He was astonished and had tons of questions for me. We reminisced a few moments. Then he asked if I would be interested in coming to his office for further discussion.

It was hard to comprehend how this Marilyn Monroe case kept coming back for more. No matter where I was or what I did, it had an uncanny ability to find me. Whatever my destiny was with this case, it was time to see it through. Deep in my heart, I always knew something was wrong, and if someone really murdered Marilyn, could that be simply ignored? I agreed to meet with him and discuss my official Coroner's investigation.

Slatzer had an office at the old Taft Building on Hollywood Boulevard and Vine. Walking up to the building entrance, I was still somewhat apprehensive about getting involved with this case again. The night before, I pulled out my old notes and refreshed my memory about the things that had happened at the Coroner's Office. It brought back deep-rooted feelings from that period of my life, and they all weren't good. Still, this was something I had to do. The time had come to talk about my experiences.

Slatzer, who told me to call him Bob, was the kind of man who could immediately put you at ease. He was very personable, with a great sense of humor and strong character to match. Bob repeated his incredible story of having been married to Marilyn Monroe. He said they loved each other as deep as anyone could love and were wed in Mexico. When the studio discovered what happened; they forced Marilyn to get an annulment.

There was no doubt Bob still loved Marilyn. He showed me pictures of them, happy and together, and explained his dedication to exposing the cover-up around her death. For him, there was absolutely no doubt in his mind that Marilyn was murdered.

He began to explain more of the evidence he had uncovered during his years of investigation. Much of it was centered on the cover-up at the house that night. Bob showed me a picture of the window that Dr. Greenson had allegedly broken to enter Marilyn's room after seeing her lying motionless on the bed. But the broken glass was on the outside. Bob claimed the window was broke from the inside of the house.

I described my experiences at the Coroner's office the morning she died, including how the studio attempted to remove her body from the crime scene. I told my story of how Dr. Curphey mishandled the case, forced me to sign the death certificate, and being set-up by that mysterious stranger.

It didn't take long for our conversation to turn towards the Kennedy's. He began to say specific things about Bobby Kennedy referenced in Marilyn's diary passages. That's when I told him there had been a journal in her property detailing her encounters with both Kennedy's and supporting many things he was saying in his book.

Bob looked at me for a moment with those eyes of his and only said,

"Describe it to me."

I told him my remembrance of the diary's appearance, and he said he had seen it before. Bob informed me that Marilyn had shared the diary with him a few weeks before she died. In his book, he wrote about some of the passages he read.

Bob asked if I knew what happened to the diary. I told him all of Marilyn's property had disappeared from the Coroner's Office, and my belief was that Dr. Curphey had taken it. He claimed two other people knew what was in the diary, Jeannie Carmine and Terry Moore. I remembered that Marilyn had mentioned them frequently in her writings.

Bob said it was common knowledge that she would write things down and that it was his belief the contents of her diary were what got her murdered. He said the wire tapers stated their surveillance devices were not the only equipment at the house. There were at least two other recording units they identified as government property. This meant the FBI and CIA were keeping tabs on Marilyn's exploits as well.

It felt uncomfortable hearing that someone killed Marilyn because of what was in the diary. In 1962, the District Attorney warned me not to discuss details about the Marilyn Monroe case, so I had never shared the information with anyone.

Bob wanted me to go public with what I knew. He said with my support as an ex-county official, we could get the Los Angeles County Board of Supervisors to reopen the case. Could you imagine me inviting the FBI, the Kennedy family, the District Attorney, the Mafia, and the CIA back into my life to create havoc again?

At this point, there wasn't much choice. I told Bob he would have my support and that I was willing to testifying how the Coroner's Office mishandled the investigation. However, Bob also knew that the contents of the diary were something I could not discuss.

"What I read in the diary must remain confidential," I told him. He agreed, paused for a moment then playfully said,

"So, what did you read?" We both laughed.

Carrying on with this would cement my destiny with Marilyn Monroe. Turning back would no longer be an option, so it was essential to get it right. We began to retrace what we knew about her case. Bob revealed additional information about the wire tapers he interviewed.

He told me about hearing audiotapes of what happened at Marilyn's house the final two days of her life. Most of what he listened to involved Robert Kennedy's conversations on Friday, August 3, and Saturday, August 4, 1962.

Bob said Marilyn's exchanges with Bobby Kennedy were very heated over those final days. There was a colossal phone argument, and on the tape, Marilyn was answering a call from Bobby Kennedy. He told her he was coming over that evening but never showed up.

The highlight of these audiotapes was Bobby Kennedy's two visits to Marilyn's house. In a state of rage, Bob heard him saying,

"I was a fool, taking you to those meetings. Where in the hell is that damn diary."

Bob said Marilyn responded with,

"The diary is mine. You weren't the first to take me to some damn meetings, but come to the press conference, you'll get a good look for yourself."

Bob said he could hear Kennedy leaving. Then, Marilyn made some phone calls, having conversations with Dr. Greenson and Jeanne Carmine.

Bob said Kennedy returned later with Peter Lawford, and he could hear someone throwing things and slamming drawers. He heard yelling from who he believed was Bobby Kennedy, saying,

"Where's that damn book, Marilyn?"

Then he described hearing a loud noise and scream that seemed to be Marilyn falling, and could also hear her crying. I told Bob that Marilyn had written about all those incidents in her diary.

Recalling what she wrote:

"They want me to call off the press conference. Too late."

"Bobby was really mad. Acted crazy and searched all my stuff. Told him it's mine. I'll never let him have it."

"Bobby came back with Peter. Shook me until I was dizzy and threw me on the bed. Should call the doctor..."

I always believed that Marilyn had made these final entries the night she died. I also told Bob about the press release that had arrived with the rest of her personal property. He said Marilyn had told him about the press conference and her plans to "blow the lid off the whole damned thing." Bob believed all of this was about Robert Kennedy. I still hadn't shared with him the depth of her involvement with the Government's Intelligence Agencies.

Bob said that while listening to that part of the tape, the wire taper told him he overheard one of the Chicago guys saying,

"We could kill her tonight and blame it on that rich boy Kennedy."

As the tape kept playing, he heard Kennedy leave the house once again. Bob said Marilyn then made several more phone calls, including another to Dr. Greenson. She asked him if he removed her bottle of Nembutal when he was there earlier. Greenson told her no, and the tape ended after that.

The wire tapers claimed the Chicago gangsters left soon after that. They told Slatzer it was never their plan to have that type of involvement. Wiretapping was one thing, but murder was another. He said they wouldn't discuss what they recorded next. Bob recounted listening to about 3 or 4 hours of these tapes and walked away, believing he had not heard everything.

He said what was on the tapes didn't sound staged, it seemed very authentic and was believable. The real test of credibility for these tapes was the voices. Bob related that he was sure it was Marilyn's voice, and Kennedy's Boston accent was easy to recognize.

I asked Bob what happened to the audiotapes of Marilyn's last night alive. He told me a New York prosecutor had confiscated Spindel's original copy as evidence. When he requested their return, they told him the tapes were lost. Why wasn't I surprised about a piece of critical evidence disappearing? Shortly after that, Bernard Spindel mysteriously died in a prison jail cell. The FBI had already taken his partner Fred Otash's copy in 1963, following President Kennedy's assassination.

"Lionel, I've never believed in fate, but I believe it was our destiny meet. We're going to let the world know what really happened to Marilyn," Bob said after our meeting. His passion was overwhelming.

Incredibly, a few months later, Jimmy Hoffa disappeared, never to be heard from again. One thing Bob and I had both seen in Marilyn's diary were her references to Hoffa.

Marilyn had written:

"I met Jimmy Hoffa at Frank's party... Sam and him were asking about Bobby..."

"Bobby was on the phone most of the night... It was something about putting that guy Hoffa in jail..."

Bob said he read some of those same passages and had also written about them in his book. He said Marilyn never fully understood who Jimmy Hoffa was and what he was involved with. In his opinion, Bobby Kennedy had put her in the middle of a crossfire that existed between Hoffa, Sam Giancana, and himself.

When the radio show featuring his interview aired, it was an enormous success. Inquiries came in from stations around the country, wanting to air the Marilyn Monroe program. We decided to produce a follow-up show, centering on Hoffa's involvement with Marilyn. We wanted to talk about the Teamsters leader's close ties to Organized Crime and how that impacted her death.

We began to schedule people to appear on the show but soon discovered there weren't many takers. The Hoffa era had made a tremendous social impact. Most people only wanted to discuss the good things Hoffa had done. We were fortunate to interview the President of Western Carloading, a trucking firm in Los Angeles. He told us a story about Hoffa using the Mafia to intimidate strike-busters and non-union workers.

The only other people who would talk about Hoffa's ties to the Mafia were a couple of representatives from the Teamsters union. One union representative told us that Jimmy Hoffa's career touched millions of workers in this country. The International Brotherhood of

Teamsters organized truck drivers and warehousemen nationwide. As the unions began to expand, they negotiated agreements to cover all employers in a given industry. This paved the way for wages that would provide workers with a comfortable middle-class lifestyle. With this came a political power that started to manifest itself in the mid-fifties.

Hoffa played a significant role in the union's skillful use of worker strikes, which eventually brought them to a position of being one of the most influential movements in the United States. The picket lines were a microcosm of America with Latinos, Asians, European immigrants, African Americans, and Whites standing shoulder to shoulder for fair wages. They didn't have to like or trust each other, but they understood the need to support each other.

The Union Rep went on to say that J. Edgar Hoover took the confrontations to a higher level by accusing the strikers of being socialist whenever commerce came to a standstill. Hoover claimed that unions and integration posed the biggest threats to America moving forward. However, there was little public support for the FBI or the multinational corporations.

This shift in public opinion was probably due to the growing evidence of Hoover's past willingness to focus considerable resources to undermine the reputation of his targets. Many more people were now aware of how the FBI gathered personal information on American citizens. They had become known for trying to destroy people like Dr. Martin Luther King and organizations such as Teamsters Union.

Another union member stated that when Hoffa accused Congress of passing strikebreaking, union-busting Bills, Senator John Kennedy responded with a full-scale U.S. Government criminal investigation of the Teamster's Union. The United States Senate established the Select Committee on Improper Activities in Labor and Management, giving them broad subpoena and investigative powers. They hired a young Robert Kennedy as the subcommittee's chief counsel and investigator, providing his first national exposure.

A strange and contentious relationship developed between Bobby Kennedy and Hoffa that would last the rest of their lives. During the show, we included the soundtrack from Kennedy's intense questioning of Hoffa at the Senate hearings, which initiated the hatred between the two men. Marilyn witnessed firsthand the Hoffa-Robert Kennedy dispute.

A few old-timers we talked to gave some insights into why they thought Kennedy, the government, and the FBI hated unions in the 1950s. In their opinion, it was because unions represented the single biggest threat to the super-wealthy power structure. If labor had a say in their wages, the playing field would begin to even out. They said Hoffa symbolized their struggle to achieve the American dream.

We were stunned by their staunch support for Hoffa, who had a known reputation of using illegal business practices, including bribery, extortion, and coercion. He was also known to have strong mafia ties. The public didn't care about that. They related to the salaries he and the unions brought into their households.

The program, which aired on stations in Detroit, Philadelphia, and Los Angeles, became the highest-rated program in the 13-year run of our series.

When the program replayed four weeks later, we asked for public opinion, and thousands responded. More than half the calls stated that the government was working for rich people and didn't care about the working class's plight.

With these programs' success, I began receiving access to national news stories on nearly every event, including new government disclosures about Marilyn Monroe. For the next ten years, all reports from the Associated Press and other international news agencies came to our production company.

My boss, Peter Newell, a Vice President with the company, encouraged the producers to cover national stories and conventions to give a minority perspective on the subject matter. Our views on Marilyn Monroe and Jimmy Hoffa were perfect examples of what he was talking about. Incidentally, Capital Cities turned would later purchase the holdings of the American Broadcasting Company, ABC Network.

CHAPTER 8:
Extra, Extra, The Empire Strikes

Nearly 15 years had passed since the death of Marilyn Monroe. Still, there hadn't been any type of big push for a new investigation. Although a few friends and some of her fans were crying foul, she was still merely a 'probable suicide' for the most part. However, the radio programs ignited a small spark, becoming a catalyst in the search for Marilyn's true cause of death.

In the time following our highly successful Hoffa show, I stepped up my investigation of the facts surrounding the Monroe case. Meeting Bob had stimulated my research efforts, primarily gathering newspaper articles, magazine clippings, and audiotapes that shed light on what I knew about the case. During that time, Bob and I would occasionally talk over the phone to compare notes and clarify details about her death.

One particular Saturday, I was conducting a production workshop for interns at KPOL-AM in Hollywood. The offices were usually empty on the weekend, so I knew most of the people who belonged there. While walking downstairs, I noticed a man who hurriedly ducked through a door. His face was not familiar, so I walked over to see if I could help him. He claimed to be a salesman for the station, there to retrieve some papers from his desk.

He then darted quickly out the back door, nothing in his hands, and left. Not thinking much, I continued with my task. About an hour later, while leaving the station, a car came across Sunset Boulevard, jumped the curb and struck the building, nearly hitting me in the process. Shaken, I watched the wrecked car back out, and it sped away.

The police were called, but could only conclude that a drunk driver ran a red light and lost control of the car. Although I filed a report, little attention was given to the fact that the vehicle failed to stop, had left the scene, and was aimed right at me. Thankfully, my athletic skills allowed me to get off the sidewalk before being planted on that car's hood. It was a terrifying situation that was way too close for comfort.

Was this something to be alarmed about or just an accident? There was no way to tell, but later that evening, another strange car was parked on my street when I arrived home. It appeared two men were sitting inside the vehicle. Maybe it was just paranoia because there wasn't any real evidence that someone was stalking me, was there? It made me wonder, who was that man I saw at the radio station earlier? He was definitely out of place.

My kids were visiting for the weekend, so I packed a few things, and we spent the night at my mother's. I had been divorced from my wife for about ten years but maintained a great relationship with my three vacation breaking youngsters. They were teenagers now and worked with me at the radio station, when possible, to cover stories for the radio program.

Lionel Jr., Crystal, and Lance, even at a young age, were veterans covering high profile stories such as Los Angeles Mayor Thomas Bradley's Inauguration and the SLA kidnapping of Patricia Hearst.

Because of their association with the show, they were fortunate to meet some of the most notable African-American figures of that time. Muhammad Ali, Andrew Young, Brock Peters, and Nancy Wilson are all people featured in television shows they helped produce.

We would get together, usually once a month, to have something we called family talks. During that time, we would discuss everything going on in our lives and share whatever feelings we had. It was a memorable time, which has kept us all incredibly close throughout the years.

We discussed the Marilyn Monroe case often during our talks, both when they were younger and since the radio program. However, things were moving fast, and I wanted them to be aware of what was happening around them. Bob was talking about trying to get a grand jury investigation, and that would have considerable implications. From what I had read in the diary, I knew there would be some ruffled feathers if the grand jury got involved. Strange things were already going on around me. If I was going to continue with this, my kids needed to know everything. That's the reason we had family talks, and that's the way we were.

After explaining things to them, my oldest son Lionel, who was at the radio station at the time of the incident, asked me a question.

"Why do you think it's so important to talk about Marilyn Monroe now?"

I thought about it for a moment before answering.

"Son, I really only have two choices. Say nothing and let the information die with me or tell the world what I know. I've been holding on to this story for a long time, but people need to hear it. It's the right thing to do."

"Well, if people need to hear it, why don't you write a book like Bob and tell your story?" My daughter Crystal asked.

"If you guys help me organize my notes and research, maybe I will," I said playfully.

However, from that point on, they wanted to know every detail of my experiences with the Marilyn Monroe case. They began to gather all my notes and organize the investigative evidence I had collected. That would become the early origins of my memoirs.

Still somewhat concerned about keeping us protected, I decided to get some advice. Captain Edward Rasheed was the man Malcolm X had introduced me to in 1962. I remembered the calming force he had been during the Watts riots as a member of the Nation of Islam's famed security force called the "Fruit Of Islam." He was someone I had become well acquainted with, working with him on several television projects for the organization. He knew everything there was to know about security. Even more importantly, I trusted him.

Although viewed as a mysterious group, the Nation of Islam acted as guardians to the African-American community. I was quite comfortable talking to Rasheed. He asked me to explain what happened. Not sure where to begin, I told him the Marilyn Monroe story and what happened at the radio station. He asked if I filed a police report, which the station had already done. Captain Rasheed told me not to worry about it and let them take care of the rest.

My investigation with Bob Slatzer was becoming more intense as the months went by. Many new details about Marilyn's death continued to surface. Bob was moving full speed ahead to get County Officials to launch a grand jury investigation into her case. During that time, I had begun producing a television show at KVST-TV 68, which was a local PBS affiliated station in Hollywood.

When Bob discovered I was producing the show, he mentioned we could receive great exposure by creating a TV show about Marilyn's case.

At the time, I hadn't thought about it much, but he was right. When I mentioned it to the team, they were ecstatic, and we set a production date.

Bob also informed me that Fred Otash, one of the men who wiretapped Marilyn's house, would appear on the program. With that revelation, all of a sudden, this had turned into something huge. Otash was a significant witness who claimed to still possess audiotapes from the night Marilyn died.

When the production day arrived, the studio was buzzing like never before. Bob arrived extra early like he always did, and we began prepping for the shoot. He mentioned being concerned that Otash hadn't answered his phone all day, but said he knew the time and location.

While getting things ready in the control booth, we began to hear a commotion in the studio. My youngest son Lance came running in.

"Dad, there's something bad happening out there," he said. I told him to wait in the booth with Bob and walked over to the door, cautiously cracking it open.

Three men had busted in and began threatening the crew, throwing chairs and waving a gun. It was unclear what they wanted because their actions were so erratic. Standing there, watching in disbelief, I saw someone tackle the man holding the gun in almost a blur, forcing him to drop it. They scuffled for a few seconds, and then all three ran out of the studio door. The scene was surreal.

Hurrying over to see if everyone was alright, I noticed it was a member of Captain Rasheed's FOI security team who had disarmed the man. Mind you, I had not mentioned this shoot to Rasheed at all. When I inquired about who told him to be here, he answered, "the Captain said you might need our help today and keep an eye on things."

We promptly called the police and turned the gun over to them. Talking to Rasheed turned out to be a smart move.

I never really understood that whole situation, and all three men evaded the authorities. After filing the police report, we never heard anything about the incident again. The truth is, only two facts remained about that entire experience. One was that we were unable to produce that television show, which would have been game changing at that time. Two, Fred Otash never showed up to the shoot and never agreed to appear again. Maybe this was just a random event, but my instincts told me it was something much more sinister. Undoubtedly, however, I was fortunate to have those protectors of the peace and thanked God for Edward Rasheed.

In 1978, I agreed to hold a press conference in Los Angeles. It was the first time my story would get publicly revealed. Although worried this would have consequences, Bob convinced me it would gain us the publicity we needed to get the grand jury involved in Marilyn's case.

We also decided to enlist Sergeant Jack Clemmons, formerly with the Los Angeles Police Department. Clemmons was the first police officer on the scene after Marilyn's death. Bob had interviewed him while writing his book, and he provided vivid details about the LAPD cover-up that took place at the crime scene. We knew that his testimony would carry weight when presenting our case to the media.

While conducting my official Coroner's investigation in 1962, I had spoken with Jack about the case. When we finally got together and talked, he remembered our conversation, saying it had always been his hope that the truth about Marilyn would get revealed. Jack always seemed like a straight shooter. He told it like it was. After all these years, speaking with him convinced me more than ever that I was doing the right thing. Our experiences with the case shared many similarities, and he, too, had a burning desire to set the facts straight.

Together, the three of us agreed to stand side by side and make the public aware of how intricate this Marilyn Monroe conspiracy was. We believed getting a grand jury investigation was an obtainable goal, and the press conference was just the beginning. The road ahead would be long for this improbable journey. Nevertheless, it was a path upon which we were all about to embark.

You can't imagine the anxiety we felt leading up to the press conference. The story I was about to reveal would accuse and possibly incriminate the former

Coroner of Los Angeles for the concealment of Marilyn's actual cause of death. Although Dr. Curphey and I had difficulties in the past, this wasn't any type of vendetta. All I wanted to do was tell the truth about how the Coroner's office handled the case. My biggest concern was the repercussions and what they would be.

The press release announced that the Deputy Coroner, who investigated the death of Marilyn Monroe, would tell the story of the inconsistencies that occurred in the Coroner's Office. Sergeant Jack Clemmons of the police department would tell why the LAPD failed to investigate evidence of a conspiracy at her house. Bob Slatzer would reveal evidence that Bobby Kennedy had been at her home the night she died and discuss Marilyn's planned press conference.

Something else also concerned me about this press conference. It was the diary. Since my Coroner's office ordeal, the only person I discussed the book with outside of my family was Bob. Although my reason for participating had nothing to do with the diary, what if the press knew about it? That possibility had to be considered, along with my response.

Since comparing notes with Slatzer, I knew more about the circumstances surrounding Marilyn's writings and the Government Agencies involved. My understanding of the things I read was much clearer. I decided to answer any specific questions about her diary. It was finally time to throw my fate into the wind.

There were about 15 or so microphones and numerous hot lights at the podium. I stood there for what seemed like an eternity as we all made statements and answered questions from the press. While cameras and tape recorders rolled, we each told our unique stories, trying to remain cool, calm, and collected.

Jack told of the LAPD's role in the cover-up and how his supervisors completely ignored his initial crime scene investigation report. He also said that key witnesses had completely changed their stories about the night's events. Jack mentioned that upon his arrival at the scene, the housekeeper, Eunice Murray, had told him that the body was found at 12:30 am. When detectives did their follow-up report, that time was changed to 3:30 am.

Jack also revealed she was in a room with numerous empty pill bottles on the bedside table. The two doctors, Greenson and Engelberg, and the housekeeper all told different stories about the night's events and appeared nervous. It was my first time hearing details about the bedroom where they discovered the star since no police report was part of my official case files.

Jack went on to say that when he arrived at the house, he noticed Marilyn was lying face down in the bed and had been dead for some time. Deputy Coroner Danbacker had also reported her time of death being incorrect and observed evidence suggesting someone moved the body. That information never was noted in the preliminary autopsy or Suicide Team reports.

Jack stated that when he made his report available to his superiors, they disregarded his observations. When he broke LAPD policy and told a news reporter what he knew, he was suspended and later fired.

Bob responded to all questions about the Kennedys' involvement in her case. He revealed what he knew about the wire tapers and discussed his close relationship with Marilyn. His disclosure about Robert Kennedy being at her house the night she died dominated the press conference. Bob had written extensively about Marilyn's connection with the Kennedys, and members of the news media had questions. He also talked about Marilyn's planned press conference and discussed the existence of her diary. Bob told the press he had seen the book, and that's what she was going reveal before she died.

My account of the activities within the Los Angeles County Coroner's Office brought into scrutiny the Coroner's handling of the case. In my statement, I discussed Dr. Curphey's treatment of the investigation, missing police reports, changing of medical documents, and the Suicide Investigation Team's findings.

The press wanted to know why I signed a death certificate declaring Marilyn's death to be probable suicide. I described how Dr. Curphey demanded I sign off and close the case. That announcement seemed to catch everyone off guard and perhaps set the tone for things to come.

Although a little nervous, I felt comfortable answering questions about the case of Marilyn Monroe, and what happened at the Coroner's Office. Finally, a reporter asked whether Jack or I had seen Marilyn's diary. Jack said no, but my response was that we logged in her diary as property at the Los Angeles County Coroner's Office. I told them her diary was in my possession while conducting the official investigation, having read parts of it during that time.

The reporter quickly followed up with what was in the diary. I explained she made numerous references regarding John Kennedy, Robert Kennedy, and U.S. Intelligence Agencies. I told them Marilyn wrote many pages about her experiences with them, but nothing implicating any conspirators in her murder.

After the press conference, I left for home, emotionally drained. My experience in front of the news media had been incredibly intense. As expected, reporters began calling the Coroner's Office for their response. Dr. Curphey had retired as Chief Coroner in 1967, and Dr. Noguchi had replaced him. Noguchi couldn't deny my assessment of the facts and choose to talk about the case based upon the Suicide Investigation Team's evaluation. He couldn't explain why so many documents had changed, how Marilyn's tissue samples had disappeared, or why Dr. Curphey had ordered me to close the case.

Most local television stations and newspapers ran stories on the press conference but didn't mention much about the Kennedy connection. Broadcast networks and national publications didn't mention them at all. Bob was extremely disappointed. Exposing Robert Kennedy's involvement with Marilyn was central to him. Bob believed it was that immersion that got her killed.

During the next few days, I kept a low profile and took some time to evaluate what had just happened. My oldest son Lionel, who attended the press conference, called saying how surprised he was about the high amount of coverage it received. I remember telling him that being in the spotlight was something I never anticipated. The entire situation left me with mixed thoughts. The truth of the matter was that if the whole thing had gone away right then and there, I wouldn't have been mad at all. However, little did we know that the press conference had lit the fuse. Our story was about to explode nationwide.

About a week later, Bob called incredibly excited. He told me the producers of the hit series "In Search Of" had called and wanted us to appear on the program. It was the number one television newsmagazine in the country, with widespread international appeal. It was a momentous opportunity to get national exposure for Marilyn's case.

Bob, Jack, and myself were interviewed on the circumstances surrounding her death and about the Kennedys' involvement in the cover-up. We each told our stories in as much detail as possible. For the first time, I provided elaborate information about Marilyn's diary, what was in it and how it disappeared from the Coroner's office. They dedicated the entire episode to Marilyn Monroe's death.

Leonard Nemoy, of Star Trek fame, hosted the program, and as it turned out, was a friend of the Kennedy family. He objected to the Robert Kennedy implications and demanded it edited out. The producers bowed to Nemoy's demand, and the references never aired. The episode, however, was an enormous hit. "The Death of Marilyn Monroe" was one of the highest-rated episodes ever for the "In Search Of" series. However, it was apparent that the Kennedy family's influence still packed a powerful punch.

Interview requests began flooding in from news media around the world. I had never quite realized the full extent of Marilyn's popularity across the globe until then. Even the Italian Television Network traveled halfway across the globe just to interview us. Our story had gone worldwide in the blink of an eye.

Quite naturally, The National Enquirer was the first news publication to show interest in the Marilyn-Robert Kennedy love affair. They requested Bob and me grant them an interview discussing the facts surrounding her death, Kennedy's involvement, and what was in the diary. Although Bob was elated, I had doubts about giving them my story. Most people considered National Enquirer, a tabloid magazine, and my goal was never to make this a gossip story. Most of the people I knew did not hold the publication in high esteem. However, this was obviously important to Bob, so I granted the interview.

Our campaign had created quite a stir with the public. All of Marilyn's friends and acquaintances called the Coroner, Police, and District Attorney, demanding a new investigation into her death. I had not realized that when Bob Slatzer found me, a missing part of the puzzle appeared. I gave his research the added credibility needed to be heard by County officials. With a Deputy Coroner set to testify on the Coroner's role in the cover-up, the grand jury would have no choice but to open the case.

In the midst of all this, someone claiming to be former Deputy Coroner Danbacker called Bob. The man had a heavy European accent, as did Danbacker, and had apparently been following the attention we were receiving. He claimed to have been in hiding and had something important for our investigation.

When I told Bob how significant of a role he had played, his ears perked up. Danbacker was the one that brought her property into the Coroner's Office and had spent three or four hours searching her house for medical information. The diary and press release were part of the property he retrieved from the house.

The only person on the staff who might have been able to put a little light on Marilyn's personal property was Deputy Coroner Danbacker. I often wondered what else he may have seen in the house, and how much he knew about what was in the diary. He would've had to look inside the book to determine its relevance.

Bob told me Danbacker sounded nervous and asked if any money was available. Bob thought he was talking about the diary, but said he never was specific. They arranged a meeting near Bakersfield, which is about 100 miles north of Los Angeles, and Bob made the drive to meet with him. Arriving at the location, he turned onto a dirt road, which led to a section of oil pumps. There were some workers and trucks in the area, so he parked near a pump and got out.

After awaiting his arrival for more than an hour, it started to get dark, and Bob said he began to get nervous. The workers in the area were leaving, and he noticed a car parked down the road. He thought it might have been Danbacker, but two men stepped out and began talking. Shortly after, another vehicle pulled up and parked behind them. These men didn't have uniforms on or fit the image of workers in the oil field. Bob said he left and drove back to Los Angeles, wondering what had just happened and looking in the rearview mirror to see if anyone was following him. He never heard from this man claiming to be Danbacker again.

Los Angeles County Officials began taking note of our claims. I was formally requested to share my story at a hearing in front of the Los Angeles County Board of Supervisors. They had become interested in Marilyn's case and were considering requesting an official grand jury investigation. It was what we all had been working to achieve. The County Board of Supervisors oversaw the activities of the Los Angeles County Coroner and had the power to get a grand jury convened. After presenting my story to them, the Board thanked me for coming forward and voted to begin the process for opening a grand jury investigation to determine the facts.

However, something funny happened along the way. Los Angeles District Attorney John Van de Camp decided to initiate his own Marilyn Monroe Inquiry, independent of the County Supervisors. Van de Camp, who was aware of the eminent grand jury investigation at the time, made the announcement less than a week after I spoke to the Board.

In 1962, the Los Angeles District Attorney's office warned me not to mention the book to anyone. Now I had told everything to the County Board of Supervisors. Hoping this was just some strange coincidence, I called Bob to see what he knew about it. He said the word is out that Van de Camp wants to take control of this investigation and the grand jury will wait to see what he concludes.

I had jumped right back in the frying pan, and the fire was on high. I knew the DA's office had no intention of saying the Coroner's Office ever was in possession of a book containing information on Marilyn Monroe's death. So why were they opening this Threshold Inquiry? Were they trying to cover-up the cover-up? Things were getting out of control, and there was no way to be prepared for what was coming next.

John Van de Camp assembled a team of investigators led by his highly touted Assistant District Attorney Ronald 'Mike' Carroll. The group began making arrangements to speak with all key witnesses, who were involved with Marilyn's case, including me.

Almost immediately, swarms of reporters converged on my house, their news trucks completely shutting down the neighborhood. The D.A.'s Office had wrongfully released sealed documents from my criminal case in 1962. They made all case evidence against me available to the media, mounting an all-out assault on my credibility.

Just like in 1962, the media had a field day while presenting this one-sided story. KNBC in Los Angeles ran it locally on their evening newscast, and it seemed as if everyone I knew saw it. Although most people understood the type of person I was and supported me, the impact was still hurtful. Bob suggested we hold a press conference to offer my side of the story, which was something I didn't want to do. That criminal case in 62' was a life-changing incident thought buried forever. It was my only criminal encounter with the law, and those records officially sealed since 1969.

Years earlier, Bob had told me that threats were made against his life and character if he included details about Marilyn's involvement with the Kennedys in his book. Perhaps I should have paid better attention to what he was saying. There was a sense of uneasiness real or imagined that I could not ignore while being involved with this highly sensitive case. Now I was about to come face to face with a Los Angeles District Attorney, who obviously had it in for me. Add to that my recent life-endangering encounters, I could only conclude that my situation was extremely precarious.

CHAPTER 9:
The District Attorney

The Los Angeles District Attorney's office began their inquiry to investigate the possible murder of Marilyn Monroe by a person or persons unknown. Some twenty years after her death, because of the publicity we created, Assistant District Attorney Ronald Carroll was commissioned to determine whether a homicide investigation was justified. His proclaimed mission was to uncover all the facts surrounding Marilyn's death.

Most people were happy about this D.A. inquiry, but my feelings were understandably different. Think about it. If the District Attorney's office didn't want me to talk about the diary in 1962, they didn't want the truth. Even more significant, if Carroll knew the real story, what would he do with it?

To be honest, this D.A.'s inquiry had caught me completely off guard. Our aim had always been the grand jury, and it never dawned on me that I could end up right back in front of the District Attorney. Obviously, the fact that nearly twenty years had passed made no difference.

Bob convinced me that a press conference would be in my best interest. He said a private investigator from the Nick Harris Detective Agency, named Milo Speriglio, had uncovered some FBI disclosures on the wiretaps at Marilyn's house. We could issue a joint press release and combine the press conference to serve both purposes.

We held the press conference a few weeks later. Telling my story about why I left the Coroner's Office was very difficult. The press grilled me, but fortunately, Speriglio's wiretap information diverted some of the questions. Afterward, a Deputy District Attorney from Ronald Carroll's inquiry team approached and said they needed to speak with me. He asked could I meet with them for lunch at the Los Angeles County Criminal Courts Building to answer some questions.

Although completely shocked at being asked, I agreed and left to meet with him after the press conference. Upon arriving downtown, three distinguished-looking individuals greeted me and said to follow them.

We went to a place I can only describe as the dungeons of the Court House. The interview room looked like a place for conducting hardcore interrogations. It was dark and surrounded by glass behind which people could watch or tape the proceedings. Quite frankly, it looked like something out of the movies.

There was no hint of coffee or tea or anything that represented lunch. It was kind of intimidating, but not wholly unexpected. It was evident they hadn't forgotten about 1962, and I felt all this was to let me know. I sat there alone in the room for a good while before anybody came in.

Sitting there was one of the coldest experiences of my life. The thoughts running across my mind were out of control. Finally, the door opened, and three men walked in. Shutting the door behind them, they stood there and looked at me. After the silent pause, one of them walked over and introduced himself as Assistant District Attorney Ronald Carroll.

Carroll was a man with a strange combination of intensity and humor. From the moment he walked into the interrogation room, it was apparent he didn't like me. Carroll's overall attitude was testy, but he readily joked with the two men sitting beside him. They designed the whole situation to intimidate and put me on edge. But I had seen it all before. When I was 22 years old, it was easy to be bullied by a District Attorney with a hidden agenda. However, things were different now. No matter what tricks they pulled out of their sleeves, I was telling the truth about what happened to Marilyn, and if there were consequences to that, so be it.

They asked multiple questions about the activities that transpired at the Coroner's Office. We went over why it was my belief her death wasn't suicide. He showed me the revised version of Marilyn's case files, which disputed much of what I said. Looking at the documents, the first thing I noticed was the misspelling of many of the Deputy's names, and some did not work for the Coroner's Office 1962. I pointed that out to Carroll and told him it was not the original paperwork from Marilyn's case.

Taking the documents back from me, Carroll said,

"I'll check on that, but these are the files we have."

I told Carroll about the diary and its contents. He said the original D.A.'s report quoted Dr. Ralph Greenson, Dr. Myron Engelberg, and others, saying they never saw a diary. They also doubted whether, in her final months, especially, Monroe was capable of keeping one.

Carroll told me that in his opinion, there wasn't any reason to believe a diary ever existed. A little irritated, I snapped back at him, saying not only did the journal exist, but I provided DA investigators this same information twenty years ago. Check your records, I told him, but don't sit there and say there isn't any reason to believe a diary existed.

Perhaps a little stunned by my mini tirade, he replied,

"We are going to get to the bottom of this."

The situation more than aggravated me. We had come too far for this type of treatment. Mr. Carroll needed to understand what the facts were, and his attitude did not even matter at this point. There was no control over what he would do with the information, but I was going to make sure he heard it. The rest was up to him.

When the interview was complete, I was asked not to mention what we discussed until after the final investigation. One of the investigators asked would I be willing to take a lie detector test, which I agreed to. My lawyer requested them to submit a list of questions as a condition of me taking the polygraph. The investigators never responded and scheduled no test.

Sergeant Jack Clemmons also visited the District Attorneys Office during the inquiry. Jack informed us that Carroll and his investigators harassed him the entire time he was there. Jack tried to tell his account of how the housekeeper changed her story, but they claimed firmly he misunderstood her. They acted as if he was incompetent. Jack told us at one point, an investigator joked that maybe he was hallucinating. Carroll said they didn't place much weight on his statements because he wasn't a trained LAPD homicide investigator and had no experience in suicides.

Jack said he left the D.A.'s office thinking the Inquiry was a sham, and the District Attorney wasn't seriously trying to investigate Marilyn's death. He believed they already had their minds made up, and the interviews were just a formality. Jack, severely shaken by his experience at the Inquiry, never expected the treatment he received. We both managed to have a little laugh when I shared with him my experience.

The next witness was another man I first met in 1962, Los Angeles County Deputy District Attorney, John Miner. He had been the first to notify Dr. Curphey of problems in Marilyn's cause of death. Miner informed investigators of what he told Dr. Curphey after meeting with her psychiatrist Dr. Ralph Greenson, who said to him that Marilyn would not have committed suicide. Miner claimed that Greenson played audiotapes for him that Monroe made in the days before she died. What he heard proved to him the actress was anything but suicidal. However, Greenson played these recordings with the condition Miner would never reveal their contents.

Subsequently, Miner refused to disclose what was on the tapes, and Carroll concluded his statements did not warrant further investigation. The resulting report stated that Miner's accounts would be omitted from the final report because of discrepancies and unanswered questions.

As the investigation continued, the District Attorney spoke with numerous witnesses and experts while trying to gather what they called 'relevant facts.' Carroll acknowledged that crucial evidence had been destroyed, leaving many questions unanswered. Monroe's internist, Dr. Hyman Engelberg, told the D.A.'s investigators that he had prescribed the medications that could have killed her.

But the fact remained that none of the medications brought from Marilyn's house that Dr. Engelberg prescribed was in her body. They asked no questions about how the police handled the many drug containers found at her home, nor why they arrived at the Coroner's Office empty. No answer as to where they came from or who brought them into Marilyn's room. More importantly, who had tried to get the body away from her house to hide the facts?

Most of the people who came forward with Marilyn's death did so willingly, although some did not wish to get involved. The only public officials willing to make statements to the Inquiry were Jack Clemmons, John Miner, and myself. Together, we represented the Police Department, District Attorney, and Coroner's Office for the County and City of Los Angeles. All three of us agreed that a cover-up had taken place and that it involved each of these departments. All of us had witnessed evidence blatantly ignored, mishandled, changed, or manipulated during the original investigation. Most importantly, all of us had reached the same conclusion; Marilyn Monroe did not commit suicide.

A few months later, Carroll and the District Attorney's Office issued a 30-page report stating in part:

> "Our inquiries and document examination uncovered no credible evidence supporting a murder theory."

Despite all the testimonies, Carroll said he did not find any credible evidence that the Coroner's Office was ever in possession of a diary. He placed little or no weight to the fact that key witnesses changed their story to officers nor that Marilyn's psychiatrist had informed a Deputy District Attorney that she was not suicidal.

The DA investigators made several reports on Marilyn's relations with the mafia. One member of the team, Frank Hronek, believed she was murdered and suspected Sam Giancana and Johnny Roselli were involved with her death. In one report, he wrote, "Marilyn might have been killed to keep her silent, and further investigation was necessary."

His final conclusion said, "Associating herself with the mafia was dangerous because of her connection with the Kennedys." Despite the fact this was Carroll's investigator making the claim, he chose not to pursue it any further.

Carroll concluded that a murder of Monroe, fitting the known facts of her death, would have required a massive conspiracy. The District Attorney review found that Marilyn Monroe acted alone in her suicide, and there was no evidence to support that anyone assisted her.

Four months after the investigation began, John Van de Camp, who was running for State Attorney General, closed down the probe. Not surprisingly, one of the largest contributors and supporters to his election campaign was Senator Ted Kennedy. Van De Camp went on to win the election and became State Attorney General. The Marilyn probe, buried, along with our hopes for a grand jury investigation.

Once again, the circumstances surrounding Marilyn Monroe's death found themselves swept under the rug. This Inquiry, along with the other investigative probes, became just another part of the massive conspiracy to cover-up evidence her case. It seeks to hide a cast of characters that includes the involvement of President John Kennedy, Attorney General Robert Kennedy, FBI

Director J. Edgar Hoover, C.I.A. operatives James O'Connell and Robert Maheu, Teamster Leader Jimmy Hoffa, Mafia Leader Sam Giancana, Dr. Myron Engelberg, and Dr. Ralph Greenson.

Bob, Jack, and I were extremely disappointed at the way all of this had unfolded. The Inquiry and everything that happened leading up to it had been a gut-wrenching experience. Over the next few months, my head became filled with confusing thoughts about everything that had transpired. I was ready for Marilyn Monroe to go away once more, and getting things back to normal.

Not surprisingly, Bob wasn't going to let that happen. In fact, he seemed to be feeling somewhat optimistic about our situation. He insisted if he laid this investigation out once more in front of the County Board of Supervisors, we could still persuade them. They could decide to bypass the District Attorney's Office and request the grand jury investigation.

Bob began to assemble what he called the Marilyn Files. He began compiling every bit of evidence or information associated with Marilyn's death into one comprehensive investigation. Bob already owned, what looked to be, the largest collection of material anywhere relating to Marilyn's case. He planned to create one concise report containing the most up to date facts and present it to the Board.

Although I never fully understood why Bob was on this crusade, you had to admire his work ethic. His best-selling book, "The Life and Curious Death of Marilyn

Monroe" was the best literary work available during that time. Bob was a true champion for Marilyn, who would never rest until he achieved justice, and never would he give up the search for new evidence.

Bob talked about discovering a man named James Hall, who claimed to have driven an ambulance that visited Marilyn's house the night of her death. Hall worked for Schaffer Ambulance Service and allegedly arrived at the scene after responding to a radio call.

Upon his arrival at her house, James Hall claimed the team found Marilyn lying on the bed face up. He said they quickly moved her to the floor, slightly dropping her in their haste then beginning to apply CPR. At that point, he insists Marilyn was still alive, but this is where his account got strange.

Hall told a perplexing story about a man, claiming to be Marilyn's doctor, who arrived and injected some kind of serum into her heart with a syringe. The doctor, who he later identified as Ralph Greenson, then pronounced her dead and told the ambulance team they could leave. Having worked numerous emergency cases, Hall said the CPR was working and could have saved her.

James Hall took two or three lie detector tests to validate his claim. According to Jack Clemmons, one of the tests was with the so-called creator of the polygraph machine. Hall passed all these tests. In a recorded interview, Schafer's Ambulance Service owner also confirmed that one of their vehicles was sent to the house that night to pick up Mrs. Monroe. Her neighbors also validated this account.

I was never sure about Jim Hall's story, although we spoke about the incident a few times. Having seen Marilyn's body and talking with John Miner and Dr. Noguchi, there was no evidence of a needle mark on her chest. However, to my knowledge, only Noguchi and Miner were at the autopsy. The way this case had gone thus far, anything was possible.

One thing was certain; this scenario could also account for there being no poison left in the stomach. It also magnifies the importance of Marilyn's tissue samples being destroyed by Dr. Abernathy under orders from Dr. Curphey. These samples could have provided concrete evidence of what really killed her.

As Bob began to develop the Marilyn Files, the first thing he did was connect the updated evidence with the chain of events for that night.

Eunice Murray, the housekeeper, first told Sergeant Jack Clemmons that she discovered the body at about 12:30 am. She later told LAPD detectives and the Coroner's Office that time was 3:30 am. Murray reported awakening, then seeing Marilyn's light on and becoming alarmed upon discovering the door was locked. She then called Dr. Greenson. When he arrived, they broke her bedroom window, climbed in, and found she was dead.

Dr. Greenson removed the phone from Marilyn's hand, immediately calling Dr. Engelberg and Peter

Lawford. According to the official police report, at 3:45 am Dr. Engelberg arrived to find Marilyn face down on the bed and pronounced her dead at 3:50 am. According to Clemmons' story, there were at least 4-5 hours unaccounted for between when Mrs. Murray found Marilyn and the doctors called the police. It wasn't until 4:25 am that they called the Los Angeles Police Department about the death. Clemmons said, after taking their initial statements, he asked the doctors why it took so long to notify the police. Their answer was they had to inform the movie studio first.

The police investigation into the death of Marilyn Monroe began like a routine inquiry into an unnatural death. Sergeant Clemmons started by examining the bedroom. According to this veteran LAPD officer, everything in her room appeared staged. He specifically noticed how the prescription bottles and her body seemed skillfully placed.

Jack was also very familiar with overdose fatalities, and knew bodies would always contort from the convulsions that come with this type of death. That wasn't the case with Marilyn. Her body was lying very naturally on the bed, appearing as if deceased for an extended period of time. In Jack's opinion, as a trained officer of the law, the whole room, or crime scene as he called it, looked "out of place." After obtaining statements from everyone present, he left when detectives arrived, and Sergeant R.E. Byron eventually assumed responsibility.

Byron overlooked significant contradictions and gaps in the witnesses' stories. Physical evidence at the scene was utterly ignored, including lifted fingerprints and photos. The entire basis of what happened that night seemed premised on statements made by Dr. Greenson, Dr. Engelberg, and housekeeper Eunice Murray. According to Clemmons, when he arrived at the house that early Sunday morning, these three were acting extremely suspicious and had a difficult time getting their story straight.

Finally, the body arrived at the Coroner's office, but not before the studio tried to get it released to the mortuary without being examined by the Coroner. The preliminary toxicology report found 30 Nembutal pills in her throat, but none in her stomach. That report later changed along with other vital documents. Then there was the rush to close the case by Los Angeles County Coroner Dr. Theodore Curphey and, of course, the removal of Marilyn's diary, containing all her notes about the Kennedys, CIA, FBI, and the mafia.

When Bob finished assembling these Marilyn Files, the information was overwhelming. In 1985, he presented his report and petitioned the L.A. County Board of Supervisors to re-open the inquiry into Marilyn's death.

Slatzer's passionate plea to the Board of Supervisors was powerful. Board Members also heard written statements from one of Marilyn's best friends, Jeanne Carmine. In 1982, Carmen spoke to Ronald Carroll's investigators during the D.A.'s Inquiry and provided them a detailed account of Marilyn's diary.

Jeanne Carmine had seen the book and told investigators how Marilyn had shared many intimate details about her writings. Carmen said the diary contained sensitive information about Marilyn's relationship with both Kennedys, along with her involvement with the Central Intelligence Agency. She was aware of the meetings between John Kennedy and Mafia members, from entries in the diary.

Carmine claimed the diary posed a major threat to Marilyn and others. Her love affair with Bobby Kennedy was all she wrote about in her final days. Carmine also described the evening Kennedy, Marilyn, and herself were at Monroe's house, and Kennedy discovered the diary. She claimed he examined it and became upset. He told Marilyn never to put anything in writing and to throw the book away. Carmine stated that Kennedy did not take the diary. Moreover, she did not know what Monroe did with it.

Surprisingly, Ronald Carroll omitted Jeanne Carmine's statements from the final Inquiry report. Other than Bob and myself, this was the first time someone had come forward and testified that Marilyn had documented the last years of her life. Now three people were telling of her association with the CIA and other federal agencies. In all of our opinions, this well-constructed book revealed more than just a failed relationship with the Kennedys.

Carmine and Slatzer both knew Marilyn when she was alive and had seen the diary. The Los Angeles County Grand Jury received an official recommendation to launch a preliminary investigation into the facts surrounding Marilyn's death. When the request arrived to the Grand Jury body, they unanimously agreed to begin a new inquiry.

Hearing that news was a remarkable feeling. After all, we had endured through this unbelievable process. Each of us felt a sincere sense of satisfaction, and nobody was more thrilled than Bob. When I saw him, the smile on his face lit the room, and I was happy for him.

Grand Jury foreman Sam Cordova launched the preliminary investigation, which would determine whether a full-scale investigation was warranted. Cordoba looked at evidence no other public official would ever touch and asked questions about the contradictory statements that witnesses had given. Cordova looked like a knight in shining armor for Marilyn's justice.

The Grand Jury Foreman scheduled a press conference and made this announcement,

"There is enough evidence to substantiate a special prosecutor to work with the Grand Jury on the investigation. The Grand Jury has never done a full-scale investigation. People have not testified under oath, and that should have happened a long time ago. It should have taken place in 1962."

However, the D.A.'s Office had other ideas once again. Ira Reiner was the newly elected District Attorney. In an unprecedented action, he removed Grand Jury Foreman Sam Cordova from his position, effectively firing him. No grand jury foreperson in California history ever was removed from office. It was a move that sent political vibrations around the country.

In addition to that, Ira Reiner announced the District Attorney's office would once again launch an independent investigation. One of Reiner's investigators contacted me and asked would I come to their office. As incredible as it seemed, I was heading back in front of the District Attorney once again.

"Returning to the District Attorney's office was the last thing I wanted," I thought as I entered the building and walked up to their office. However, everything seemed like it was crumbling once again, and if talking to the D.A. could help, it was worth a try. Still, I could not forget the treatment received a few years earlier by one of Reiner's predecessors, so my guard was definitely up.

The second interview took place in the District Attorney's Office, where at least there was sunlight. Things were completely different this time.

"Thanks for coming, Mr. Grandison" is how they greeted me.

The D. A. investigators were now giving some attention to my claim that Marilyn Monroe kept a journal. They were aware of what Jeanne Carmine had said and wanted to know more about the contents of this mysterious book.

Reiner's investigator was very polite and listened attentively to my story.

"Don't worry, Mr. Grandison, you're going to get your investigation," he said as he helped me put on my coat when I prepared to leave.

Leaving the office, I felt extremely positive about our situation. Maybe, Ira Reiner wanted to clean up the D.A.'s office and give Marilyn Monroe the investigation she deserved. However, that was not to be the case.

The next day newspaper headlines read,

"New Marilyn Probe Nixed by D.A."

And just like that, everything was over.

I had to come to grips with the fact that the cover-up was still in full effect. Someone didn't want the public or anyone else to know the depths of this matter. With the Kennedy's, CIA and the FBI involved, any official public investigation into the Marilyn Monroe's death was doomed by the so-called massive conspiracy theory from the start. No witnesses, testimony, or evidence were deemed credible or viewed as fact with these power brokers.

For all intent and purposes, this was the end of law enforcement's attempt to uncover the truth. There were more promises of District Attorney Reviews and mutterings of convening a grand jury. Not surprisingly, even as County officials stopped their investigation, new

information was beginning to surface from the FBI and
CIA.

CHAPTER 10:
Far-Reaching Ramifications

When Ira Reiner fired the grand jury foreman and shut down the investigation, it closed the door on the last chance to determine the conspirators in Marilyn's death. The opportunity to acquire sworn testimony from all of the key witnesses still alive would never come again. In the months and years that followed, little or no activity was taking place on the Marilyn front.

During that time, with my now-adult sons' help, I began to assemble my memoirs. All of my information and notes were transferred to a device replacing my typewriter, called a personal computer.

Although new information was continuing to come out, many of my notes from the diary remained were unclear. Names like Iron Bob, Big Jim, and Eduardo still didn't have faces. Slowly I began to learn more.

During the mid-eighties, the BBC produced a documentary about Marilyn Monroe. While watching, I saw an old film clip of President Achmad Sukarno of Indonesia getting off a plane. I remembered that Marilyn had made entries about him in her diary.

Marilyn wrote:

"Big Jim wanted me to do a job for them. They were trying to bring down a

foreign leader who doesn't want to cooperate."

Jim O'Connell of the CIA's Far East Office contacted Marilyn about doing a series of sexy photos in Hollywood and two New York hotels. In 1962, the agency was actively trying to discredit Sukarno, believing there was a real danger that Indonesia would fall to the Communists.

The documentary stated that CIA documents revealed a scheme using Marilyn to discredit Sukarno. Knowing him to be a ladies' man, they brought him to Hollywood, arranging an extravagant dinner and reception with some movie stars invited.

Among those invited by the CIA was Marilyn Monroe. Her orders were to walk up to Sukarno, throw her arms around him and play the sexy dumb blonde. Marilyn had been carefully briefed and instructed to appear at the affair in a low cut dress. It went further than just Jim O'Connell asking her to do the Agency a favor. Briefings are for individuals working on assignments or used in military terms—debriefing is passing on information to higher-ups that operatives have obtained.

The director of the CIA at that time, John McCone, stated on public television in February 1989, how all operatives get briefed and the extent to which the agency would go to influence foreign governments. McCone, handpicked to run the Central Intelligence Agency in

1961 by President John Kennedy, had restructured the organization since the Bay of Pigs fiasco in Cuba.

When I thought about it, she had also written in her diary about being approached by O'Connell and Maheu to do a sex film.

She wrote:

"Bob and Big Jim talked about shooting a film with Mr. Hughes to embarrass this diplomat."

It was not so far-fetched that the CIA would ask America's sex symbol to help them influence international politics. Maybe even discuss top secret information with her once they found out she was doing the same thing for the FBI.

Journalist Anthony Summers had reported a substantial effort to come up with a pornographic film, or some still photographs that could pass for Sukarno and a blond female engaged in sex. According to FBI records, when the available porno films failed to turn up an actor who could pass for Sukarno, the CIA strived to produce a movie. I discovered the outcome was a movie produced for the CIA by Howard Hughes, who worked with Robert Maheu on other intelligence operations.

Reportedly Hughes did deliver a film to O'Connell entitled "Happy Days," which starred a well-known Hollywood blond named Marilyn Monroe. The ultimate fate of the blackmail film is unknown, but a gallery owner recently found outtakes. We do know photo sessions between Marilyn and Sukarno did happen because there were eyewitness accounts of meetings in Hollywood and at a New York hotel.

Marilyn went to a higher calling after Jim O'Connell's promotion to Far East Chief Regional Security Officer. He recruited Marilyn and Robert Maheu to assist him in his secret missions. The CIA's plan for the Far East was to have some leadership changes in Asia.

All of this strong attention to third World countries had been brewing for some time. Colonialism was coming to an end in Africa and Asia. Gandhi had got the British out of India, and the Dutch and French were next in Viet Nam. Most independent countries were forming new governments and looking for allies.

In 1955, at the invitation of President Sukarno, third world leaders agreed to gather in Bandung, Indonesia. American activist Paul Robeson was involved in the conference. Representative Adam Clayton Powell of New York pleaded for the U.S. Government to attend. The CIA advised the President and Congress that the meeting was subversive because Indonesia was bringing together leaders of the decolonized peoples of Asia and Africa.

In 1961, Sukarno formed a political alliance called "The Initiative of Five." Malcolm X was a significant contributor to this movement. It was later that CIA disclosures identified Robert Maheu in the attempted murder of Malcolm in Cairo, Egypt. Malcolm was there, meeting with Egyptian President Gamal Nasser regarding his appearance at the United Nations on the Human Rights issue. The American government was not ready for the subject of Human Rights.

February 11, 1962, Robert Kennedy arrived in Jakarta in a final attempt to prevent Indonesia from moving closer to the Communist bloc of nations. We don't know if Marilyn accompanied him, but have reason to believe he had the sex film. What we do know is Sukarno was overthrown partly because of this scandal.

Marilyn attended communist meetings in Mexico after that episode. It is not confirmed, but suspected, that the CIA was behind this. They received intelligence that the Cubans were in negotiations with the Soviet Union regarding military support. This communist factor had followed Marilyn since the first pages of her diary. Was she an active government agent, communist party member, or just a showpiece on the world stage of international politics?

Almost certainly, the Kennedy White House was fully aware and informed about Marilyn's activities with the CIA. If Marilyn didn't have a security clearance, why was she there? They were discussing national security matters that would affect the future of the world. If the Cubans and the Soviets joined forces, it could mean nuclear war.

So this is not just about Marilyn Monroe's unfortunate death but her accounts relating to policymakers and bureaucrats' inner workings. The people in this story had a great deal of power as representatives of the American People. History must have a complete record of decisions and indiscretions made by these people because the government employed so many that might have benefited from her timely death. Once you follow the paper trail, the list expands rather quickly.

Remember President Richard Nixon's Watergate? There is a distinct tie-in between Marilyn's relationship with the Fair Play For Cuba Committee and the CIA break-in of Democratic Headquarters trying to get or plant Cuban documents some ten years later.

In an article entitled "Mission Impossible" by Eugenio Martinez, one of the Watergate burglars, and a Cuban, he stated,

"Cubans have never stopped fighting for the liberation of our country. I have personally carried out over 350 missions to Cuba for the CIA. I can't help seeing the whole Watergate affair as a repetition of the Bay of Pigs.

All of the agencies of the U.S. government were involved, and they carried out their plans in so ill a manner that everyone landed in the hands of Castro - like a present. Generally, I talk to my CIA case officer at least twice a week and maybe on the phone another two times. I told him right away that Eduardo was back in town.

Eduardo was a name that all of us who had participated in the Bay of Pigs knew well. He had been the maximum representative of the Kennedy administration to our people in Miami. I then learned his name for the first time, E. Howard Hunt. We talked about the liberation of Cuba, and he assured us that the whole thing is not over, and he blamed the Kennedy administration for not supporting us on the beaches of the Bay of Pigs."

When I started researching this project, the United States Government's role in Marilyn Monroe's life was a glaring factor. I had come across the name Eduardo in Marilyn's diary and made a note. However, I didn't write down any specifics.

In her diary, she wrote:

"The spy boys were really serious about killing Castro. Big Jim and Eduardo were actually involved in the Bay of Pigs..."

Marilyn was describing a meeting with Eduardo and Big Jim O'Connell, identifying them as being involved in the Bay of Pigs. This entry was part of her extensive notes about her Kennedy meetings with the CIA.

We now believe Eduardo to be the infamous Howard Hunt, of President Nixon's Watergate squad, involved in the Cuban campaign. If we opt to believe him, Eugenio puts Hunt at the side of President Kennedy in 1961. According to Marilyn, Hunt was involved in the conspiracy plot to kill Castro and participated in meetings with Jim O'Connell. Eduardo was reportedly in Mexico at the same time as Marilyn. He could have been with her in other activities such as the mysterious visit to the Cuban Embassy or Fair Play for Cuba Committee meetings.

I once asked Bob who he thought killed Marilyn, after all his investigating. He said most likely the Secret Service agents who were there or CIA under orders from Robert Kennedy. I guess my reaction was sort of revealing because Bob went on to say,

"You think that's impossible? So were the Bay of Pigs, the assassination of John Kennedy, the assassination of Robert Kennedy, The disappearance of Jimmy Hoffa, the murder of Sam Giancana, and the murder of Bernard Spindel. As a study of the unholy alliance between the Mafia and the CIA illustrates, Generals or Presidents don't ever have to pull the trigger. They just have to make the decision and live or die with it."

With that answer, there were now more suspects in Marilyn's death than in a 'Murder She Wrote' mystery. The growing list now includes the CIA, FBI, Secret Service, Mafia, Jimmy Hoffa, Dr. Greenson, Dr. Engelberg, Howard Hunt, Robert Maheu, and the Kennedys.

Marilyn was trying to match wits with some very crafty individuals. I'm sure suicide was an option once she realized her situation. Unless she wanted to be water-boarded, have her fingernails pulled out one by one, or drugged into a senseless state.

CHAPTER 11:
The Marilyn Files

In 1991, William Speckin and Mel Bergman of Producer's Video contacted Bob Slatzer about producing a project based upon his "Marilyn Files" research. They wanted him to do a video documentary, write a book, and create the television version of our investigations. This was a fitting acknowledgment of our detective work, which we all felt provided the basis for a clear analysis of those last days in Marilyn Monroe's life.

Bergman and Speckin were determined to make the facts of Marilyn's death public. According to them, their goal was to re-open the case, layout the events surrounding the controversial death, and see justice done for Marilyn Monroe. It was a massive undertaking after 30 years, but Bob convinced me to go along. Besides, there was no compensation for appearances during all this time. At least these producers were willing to cover gas money.

When Bob finished his book, appropriately called "The Marilyn Files," I was impressed with the great detail he presented. Gathering most of the people involved with the D.A. investigation and those he talked to over the years, he videotaped them for the documentary.

It was kind of exciting, offering me the rare opportunity to meet Jeanne Carmine and Terry Moore, two people I had read about in Marilyn's diary. Jeanne and Terry did not doubt Marilyn's murder. Both had seen her diary and were aware of what she had written. That meant four of the people who knew about the journal were there.

During the production, I spoke with her about the experiences we shared in this quest for Marilyn's justice. She told me it puzzled her why investigators never made her statements public, and she was here to fix that. When the subject of the diary came up, she seemed surprised by how much I knew, but by the time we finished chatting, both of us were sure we'd seen the same book.

While being taped, both Jeanne and Terry talked about the grave situation Marilyn found herself in and what they had seen or heard. Carmine mentioned that Marilyn believed her phones were being tapped and often would make her calls from payphones. That not only collaborated what Bob said about the wiretapping but also verifies Marilyn's connection to intelligence activities. How would she have known or even thought her phones tapped?

Carmine and Moore also went into great detail about what she wrote in her diary, especially regarding her love affair with Bobby Kennedy. They talked about Marilyn and Bobby's secret trips to the beach and driving around the city in disguises, caught up in their whirlwind romance.

Both women described expressing to Marilyn their deep concern for her safety when she told them about the press conference she was planning. While talking to them, I also mentioned the entry Marilyn made in her diary regarding how they felt about Dr. Greenson.

She wrote:

"Dr. Greenson spent hours with me discussing world politics."

"Jeanne and Terry think he has some kind of control over me."

Although she didn't mention Greenson by name, Jeanne Carmine told me she always felt Marilyn was around too many psychiatrists. They made her extremely insecure. Carmine told me that Marilyn was a tough woman, particularly in the last years of her life, despite her perceived image.

I also had the opportunity to see someone for the first time in nearly thirty years, former Deputy District Attorney John Miner. He elaborated on the audiotapes of Marilyn, played for him by Dr. Greenson. Miner claimed that Marilyn could be heard making plans for the future on these tapes and obviously was not suicidal. He indicated that he filed two reports stating his opinion, one with the District Attorney's office and another with the Coroner's Department. Miner told us that during the 1982 District Attorney Inquiry, investigators informed him that both reports mysteriously got lost.

This production was the largest gathering of people who knew something about Marilyn's death since the District Attorney Inquiry some ten years earlier. Others in attendance included my friend Jack Clemmons, Jim Hall, Milo Speriglio, Former Mayor of Los Angeles Sam Yorty, pathologists, forensic experts, friends of Marilyn, and of course, Bob Slatzer.

During my interview, I casually told my story as I had done so many times before. It was difficult to believe that nearly thirty years had passed since that historic day in August, which changed my life forever. While telling my story, I didn't press the issue on the other revelations of the diary. No one seemed to want to talk about how deeply she was involved with the FBI or the Communist movement, and to tell the truth, neither did I.

By now, we all knew that many people had the motive and opportunity to murder Marilyn and that she hadn't committed suicide. The diary detailed Marilyn's involvement with each of these people. Still, it was apparent our legal system was unprepared to investigate the case based upon that or any other evidence we presented. Our hope with the documentary was to keep this story alive and not let this cover-up get buried with us.

The last person to be interviewed was a forensics pathologist named Dr. J. Dewitt Fox. He had studied Marilyn's case and determined that Marilyn could not have swallowed the number of pills reported. No glass of water appeared at the crime scene, and he said it would have been impossible to ingest them all without it. He also cited that in his experience as a forensics pathologist, one of the biggest red flags in her case was that she was discovered nude. Women who fall into her category of suicides rarely are found naked. That goes completely against the psychological profile of this type of case.

After his interview, I spoke with Dr. Fox about his analysis and how he envisioned Marilyn's killing. He told me that more than likely, a suppository was used to administer the poison. He noted that if a more thorough autopsy had taken place and her organs not destroyed, it could have been easily determined.

Dr. Fox's logic made perfect sense and reminded me of a note I made about one of Marilyn's diary entries.

She wrote:

"They were discussing how to kill Castro. Johnny Roselli boasted about the mafia's ability to infiltrate anybody's security to kill them. They have a pill to cram up Castro's butt."

This quote was relating to Marilyn's meeting with John Kennedy, the CIA, and mafia members. They were talking about using a suppository on Castro. It was the most revealing evidence I discovered during this production and fueled much of my research for years to come. Let's face it; there was nobody better equipped to pull off a cover-up of this magnitude than the CIA and FBI.

The documentary concluded that the Kennedys would have gained the most from Marilyn's death. She knew of some extremely sensitive political deals that could have handicapped the Kennedy Administration and perhaps ignited an international incident. Not to mention what she knew personally about John and Bobby Kennedy.

It was never my goal to determine who murdered Marilyn. I only wanted to ascertain her real cause of death. It appeared to me that if this project could establish reasonable doubt, the investigation would stay alive. At the very least, there would be grounds to continue searching for answers and one day close out the case of Marilyn Monroe.

For the television special, "The Marilyn Files Live," they brought together a panel of Prosecutors, Pathologists, and other experts from around the country. The goal was to discuss whether there were enough contradictions to warrant a new grand jury investigation. We shot the production at Raleigh Studios in Hollywood, complete with elaborate sets.

The producers created dramatic reenactments of scenes from Marilyn's house during the LAPD investigation, as recalled by Jack Clemmons, and the same for the Coroner's Office, as depicted by my accounts. It was the first time I was able to sit down and visualize that experience. We used actors to portray ourselves and recreate the circumstances to show the cover-up in vivid detail.

"*The Marilyn Files Live*" was broadcast internationally and hosted by actor Bill Bixby of "The Incredible Hulk" fame. The two-hour special aired prime time in over one hundred cities and was seen by millions worldwide. The audience response to the show was so huge that many cities re-ran our program the following week. Producers did a marvelous job of getting together a strong cast of people who knew something about the case or had a professional opinion on how it's handling.

Most people interviewed for the documentary, participated in the television special. We all hoped that public opinion would force officials to reconsider the suicide ruling. I thought this would be an excellent way of presenting the evidence to a new generation of people interested in Marilyn's death.

They scheduled my interview with Bill Bixby during the second hour of the live telecast. We went over the questions, and I felt comfortable that the portrayal would be accurate. I was amazed at how knowledgeable Bixby was about Marilyn's case. When we spoke backstage, he was very engaging and seemed genuinely captivated by our story.

What made this event so explosive was it's live broadcast worldwide. All eyes were on us, and there were no re-takes or do-overs. Everybody was on the spot, to tell the truth as they knew it, and the public would be the judge and jury. It was no place for the weak at heart, and the program didn't disappoint.

Bill Bixby did a masterful job of hosting the show and allowing us to present our experiences. The dramatic reenactment scenes were powerful and helped capture the essence of Jack Clemmons' story and mine. Bixby asked us pointed questions based on those scenes.

Even the former mayor of Los Angeles, Sam Yorty, who was supposed to supervise the City's investigation, explained what the Los Angeles Police Department told him. As Mayor, during the time of Marilyn's death, he stated that LAPD Chief William Parker informed him that Bobby Kennedy was in Los Angeles the night of Marilyn's death. In fact, police officials knew he was staying at the Beverly-Wilshire Hotel.

Yorty also discussed how in the late sixties, he requested a copy of the Los Angeles Police Department's files on Marilyn Monroe and told none existed. Yorty went on to say he later discovered there probably was a file, but his request remained unfulfilled.

As the production went on, there were subtle changes in the mood. Prosecutors, invited by the producers, began to get aggressive in their questioning. There had been no previous indication that any questions getting asked by anyone other than the moderators.

For instance, former Deputy District Attorney John Miner found himself in front of an impressive group of former District Attorneys and prosecutors from various States and Counties. They began to go into serious interrogation with Miner while discussing the audiotapes

Dr. Greenson played for him. They asked Miner what was on the tapes that convinced him Marilyn of Marilyn's murder. He said he was not at liberty to disclose that information, but would testify if subpoenaed by the grand jury.

They accused the former Deputy District Attorney of withholding evidence. They also said criminal charges should get filed for not answering their questions. Miner was so irritated by this line questioning that when he got up to leave the interview area, his microphone was still attached. He almost destroyed the set.

I wondered how the prosecutors had convinced Mel and Bill to change the script and allow them to threaten him with prosecution during the live broadcast. Maybe it was a District Attorney thing and their way to get back at Miner for not supporting the company line in his observations. I could certainly understand that because it had also happened to Clemmons and me.

It was now apparent that all three public officials on duty at the time of Marilyn's death, claiming the possibility of homicide, had been vilified or discredited. Only John Miner, Jack Clemmons, and I were still willing and able to tell our story about what had happened in 1962. Neither Dr. Noguchi nor any other Police Officials would give comments for the program.

Afterward, everyone agreed that this was a complicated death provoking more questions than answers. In the end, we all laughed, shook hands, and wondered how this tragedy could have happened. Most of the so-called experts would say, if they had been the Coroner, District Attorney, Pathologist, or Chief of Police, this could never have happened.

I considered asking them if the White House, CIA, and FBI were advising them to keep their opinions to themselves how they would have reacted. They would have probably toed the lines just as many of these public officials did because pressures within their departments undoubtedly demanded it.

Making money for appearances on television shows was never my aim or purpose. Exposing this Marilyn Monroe cover-up was a matter of principle, and selling my interview could be perceived as personal gain. No amount of money could ever make up for what this Marilyn Monroe case cost me, but discovering the truth might help me break even.

When the Marilyn File producers wanted me to sign a personal release form, Mel said they were going to sell this on DVD and pay to use my interview. I should have known something was wrong. While writing my memoir, and going through my mounds of paperwork, I came across a check from Producer Video Inc. Stamped on it was "insufficient funds." All I could say was, "So much for getting paid."

Anyway, this television production would be the last public outcry for the truth. The eyewitnesses to the cover-up and conspiracy surrounding the Marilyn Monroe death would never come together again.

Looking back in hindsight, the one element missing from "The Marilyn Files Live" television special was a recreation of the press conference Marilyn was planning. I often envisioned her in front of the press, reading what I had seen in the diary. She was probably the only one that had the charisma to tell the story and answer the questions. Did she see herself as a scorned woman looking for revenge, or as a disgruntled agent for the CIA and FBI or just a party girl who felt used by powerful people? Like everything else that has happened since Norma Jean Baker became Marilyn Monroe, there was no answer.

To exist, Marilyn had always had to use her sexuality. It was apparent to everyone who saw her that she was something special. The Hollywood star grew up in an unstable environment. According to her accounts, men had always offered money, clothes, someplace to stay. They had promised to fulfill her many dreams since she was fifteen.

During her press conference, Marilyn may have told us how the FBI approached and requested her to perform specific assignments for "America." She might have elaborated on how a Hollywood actress was influenced with the promise of money, power, and success if she spied on somebody she knew.

According to Marilyn's diary, Roger Maheu recruited her to get information for the House Un-American Activities Committee.

She wrote:

"The FBI wanted me to do something for America. They sent Iron Bob to ask me if Arthur was a Communist."

The FBI was actively gathering personal information on American citizens. They then discreetly leaked their version to groups such as the House Un-American Activities Committee and ardent anti-communists such as Sen. Joseph McCarthy, who frequently used the unsubstantiated claims to destroy reputations or file false criminal charges.

Marilyn was the perfect operative, and they offered to fulfill all of her dreams and more. However, she didn't realize until it was too late that this path would forever dominate her destiny.

Marilyn might have also answered questions about how her introduction to John Kennedy. It would be interesting to know exactly how this happened. Would she have said Robert Maheu arranged their meeting? In the clandestine world, "Iron Bob" was involved in some of the most notorious intelligence activities of the 20th century.

Maheu was the man who CIA officials thought of when they began entertaining the idea of killing Castro in 1960. His work for the Agency was primarily covert operations, from planning the assassination of foreign and domestic targets, to gathering information on American citizens. Maheu handled the jobs in which intelligence agencies officially could not be involved.

What would Marilyn have said about her meetings with CIA agent Big Jim O'Connell and mafia members like Johnny Roselli, who was to set up a meeting with mob boss Sam Giancana to discuss killing Castro? According to her diary, Marilyn could have provided intimate details about the Government's association with the Mafia.

She may have told about the triangle formed between the Mafia, CIA, and Kennedy Administration as they began planning the downfall of Castro. Marilyn heard much of the planning and, for better or worse, wrote it down in her diary.

After marriages to Arthur Miller and Joe DiMaggio ended in divorce, John and Robert Kennedy were the focal points of Marilyn's world until her final breaths. Her accounts may have revealed details of her intimate relationship with President John F. Kennedy, who dumped her after his wife, Jackie Kennedy, discovered their relationship.

Without a doubt, however, I believe Bobby Kennedy would have dominated Marilyn's press conference. According to most accounts, Bobby initiated his relationship with Marilyn to protect his brother's marriage. The President sent Bobby to explain why he could no longer see her, but he became attracted to Marilyn. They began a steamy affair that broke all the national security rules and ultimately concluded with Marilyn's death.

These are details only Marilyn would have known and could have told if she had been allowed to hold her press conference. However, that was not the case, and Marilyn took those secrets to the grave. The world, as we know it today, might have been a little different had she been able to speak.

CHAPTER 12:
My Investigation

When first sitting down to write my memoir, I wondered what the response would be. Although most of the people who shared this experience with me have died, I richly remember their passion, and how they told a disbelieving society that Marilyn Monroe did not commit suicide. This project has allowed me to relive those experiences and recall some of my conversations with them.

We had been recorded on many shows and given many interviews about Marilyn's case. A movie trailer put on my website features statements from three investigators familiar with the circumstances surrounding her death.

One was a doctor who worked for the District Attorney's Office and was at her autopsy. Another was the first Los Angeles Police officer at her house the night she died, and the third was me, who had signed her death certificate. Two others appearing on the trailer were friends of Monroe, who talked to her in the hours before she died.

Their statements repeated testimonies given to the Los Angeles County District Attorney's Office during its 1982 Inquiry. These five people represented the leading proponents for Marilyn's murder-not-suicide theory. I received this email from an individual, who obviously was a huge Marilyn Monroe fan, and saw our movie trailer on YouTube.

Subject: Marilyn Project

FYI, you have MANY false facts in your trailer already. There are many supporters, like myself supporting and looking after Marilyn's GOOD NAME, whereby sensationalism for profit will not fly. Those days are LONG GONE.

So suggest you check your facts, sources et al, and make any literary or visual effort TRUE to Marilyn, or there is little choice but to call you out publicly via social networks, etc. which, of course, leads to POOR SALES…

Take your pick and good luck to you…

This email is indicative of the confusion that has clouded the public's perception of the facts surrounding her death. I once had a well-known journalist from the BBC call me a liar before even asking me one question. Since my involvement, many conflicting stories written about Marilyn's death have tended to cloud the truth. Disinformation has been this cover-up's most potent weapon, and in today's socially driven information network, it's strong as ever.

Now let us profile this e-mailer. He or she probably was not even alive when Marilyn died. Even if they were, they probably were not officially informed about the facts of her death. Their knowledge, likely based on her films, and stories wrote by journalists, who were more confused than they were.

To call the public officials who saw the available evidence at that time, not factual, is absurd. If they are sincere about wanting to protect Marilyn's image, I suggest they read this book. Then they will understand how Marilyn's case evolved from beginning to end, and the implications of her death. I've been part of this investigation for too long and may have forgotten more about this case than 99% of the people will ever know. So a little thing like someone not believing my story cannot dissuade me.

My investigation of 'The Case of Marilyn Monroe' has continued to be an incredible but often-intense journey through Hollywood's biggest mystery. Even since shooting the Marilyn Files, new information and adventures have continued.

In 1993, I appeared on a special edition of "Hard Copy" called Marilyn Monroe: The Last Word. This television documentary was perhaps the most controversial program ever produced on the death of Marilyn Monroe. The show featured dramatic recreations of the love affair between Bobby Kennedy and Marilyn and many other aspects of her life. Paramount Pictures put up the money to produce this documentary, which obviously cost a pretty penny, but never received wide distribution. Rumors would later surface, stating that the Kennedy's influence scuttled the project.

On the program, journalist Anthony Summer's claimed Marilyn was fully aware of her actions with the CIA. Her role in the agency was no secret. He also stated that Justice Department officials believed the Mafia murdered Marilyn Monroe in an attempt to smear the Kennedys. Summers said he was told by former FBI Assistant Director Courtney Evans to look in the direction of Sam Giancana. The documentary suggested the CIA was orchestrating this cloak of deception, which wasn't surprising at all.

Fred Otash, one of the men who wiretapped Marilyn's home, also appeared on the program. Otash made astonishing claims that Peter Lawford had contacted him the morning of Marilyn's death, frantic about what had happened that night. Lawford told him that Bobby Kennedy was there, and about the big fight. He wanted to hire Otash to help cover-up evidence at Marilyn's house.

If this statement was true, it meant that Peter Lawford had contacted the same private investigators that Jimmy Hoffa hired to bug Marilyn's house. The same men who listened to wiretaps with Mafia gangsters hired by Sam Giancana.

Bob Slatzer, who appeared on the program, was as shocked as I was to hear these claims. But such goes the ongoing drama that has surrounded this infamous case. As I look back at my investigation and everything learned, I can't help but think how fate has played such a massive role in all this.

Let me begin with being at home with my family on August 4, 1962. Little did I know that events were happening in West Los Angeles that would impact the rest of my life. Marilyn Monroe was dying, and a cast of characters was there to make sure nobody would ever discover how.

Upon arriving to work that Sunday morning and discovering someone trying to remove Marilyn Monroe's body from the scene of a crime, things would never be the same. As far as the investigative aspect of this case, I have chronicled my recollection of the facts supported by evidence. No one from the Los Angeles County Coroner's Office has ever come forth publicly with a denial of anything I've ever said.

I'm sure that Dr. Curphey was not too happy with me because I refused to let it go. He probably would have told me, "Here's another fine mess you got the Coroner's Office into." There had been rumors through the grapevine saying he thought I was a traitor to our profession and him. In his office, there was a big sign on the wall that said, 'Silence is Golden.' I always thought it was referring to the noise, but now seemed to be meant for employees.

Being the last public official willing to talk about the Marilyn Monroe cover-up, let me start with what I saw at the Coroner's Office. That is where the basis for my investigation began. My boss forced me to agree with a flawed conclusion—flawed because the investigation was incomplete and clearly rushed to the finish line.

First of all, there was no formal LAPD investigation report or even a preliminary report required by law before closing any Coroner's case. The medical information from her doctors was not verified nor supported by the facts, and toxicology reports further confused matters.

After seeing what my preliminary investigation had revealed, Dr. Curphey insisted none of it mattered. He ordered me to agree with his cause of death ruling that listed probable suicide and sign the certificate without many of the documents required. I wasn't Sherlock Holmes or even a veteran of thousands of Coroner's cases. Still, after three weeks of investigation, it was apparent that something wasn't right. She died under a much more complicated set of circumstances.

District Attorney and Grand Jury Inquiries opened and closed their investigations after minimal to no inquiries into the actual cause of death. Subsequent studies by researchers such as Robert Slatzer, Donald Wolfe, Anthony Summers, and others have given us a broader timeline than even the District Attorney or the Los Angeles Police Department. These private investigations have used FBI and CIA disclosures and testimonies by ex-officials like me to discover the truth.

There are definite links between the unfortunate murders of President John Kennedy, Senator Robert Kennedy, and Marilyn Monroe. The deaths or disappearances of many people involved in this case have led us to conclude something is missing. It is crystal clear that some individuals or agencies associated don't want the truth to be known. They have blocked all official Investigations, and anyone who didn't comply was discredited or worse.

Friends and family are left to figure out what happened. The Kennedys were a powerful family with money and influence. Perhaps they were able to discover the facts surrounding the deaths of their loved ones despite the cover-up. Marilyn Monroe had no known relatives. In her case, the conspirators probably thought they could keep everyone quiet, thus leaving the American public to draw its conclusion.

Every conceivable step was taken to make the cover-up work. The FBI gobbled up evidence that the CIA paid journalists to hide their involvement, and the Kennedy White House blocked all other media coverage. From the first hours of this assignment, the people at Marilyn's house made a strong attempt to report inaccurate information. It has been almost impossible to sort out the truth.

The hard evidence supports that Marilyn Monroe died either by accidental overdose or was assassinated by a person or persons unknown. If you want to know why other public officials didn't concur, you need to understand that these people had jobs. They yielded to the intense pressure, precipitating the highly sophisticated cover-up that followed.

For instance, the housekeeper Eunice Murray, who discovered Marilyn's body, was a nurse assigned to

Marilyn's care by her psychiatrist, Dr. Ralph Greenson. Evidence suggests that as many as seven hours may have elapsed before calling the authorities the night Marilyn died. Credible sources have stated her body traveled to a hospital during the interim and later returned to the house.

Walter Schaefer, owner of the Schaefer Ambulance Service, was recorded saying they dispatched an ambulance to Marilyn's home. He claimed his company's paramedics transported her to Santa Monica Hospital. Then they returned her body to the house, placing it in her bedroom. Evidence also points to several additional people present at Marilyn's home during that time.

Bob told me he spoke with Inez Melson, Marilyn's business manager. She stated that four representatives from 20th Century Fox were present during those early morning hours. Melson claimed the studio personnel removed anything that could tarnish Marilyn's reputation.

The most compelling part of my investigation has been the journal or diary allegedly written by Marilyn Monroe. In her own words, she wrote the accounts of the last seven or eight years of her life. This book disappeared from the safe at the Los Angeles County Coroner's Office two days after a deputy brought in. Maybe County or Government officials removed the book to take it out of circulation, or perhaps the motive was all about money. We may never know.

My investigation shows that around 7:00 pm on Saturday, August 3, Robert Kennedy, Peter Lawford, and two Secret Service Agents visited Marilyn. Kennedy was adamant about finding the book. On the wire tapper's audiotape, heard by Bob Slatzer, he described a fight that turned violent. Slatzer heard Peter Lawford saying,

"Marilyn, Marilyn, give him what he wants."

She started screaming, and Bob heard what sounded like a loud slap and someone falling. Peter then told Robert Kennedy,

"We better get out of here. Someone might have heard this commotion."

Slatzer heard the door slam, and Marilyn crying in the background. He thought Bobby said, "Give her something to calm her down." Even though it sounded off mike and muffled, he was inclined to believe that's what was said.

Peter Lawford and Bobby Kennedy left Marilyn's house at about 8 PM, and Lawford took him to the airport. Some witnesses claim to have talked to her between 8:00 and 10:30 PM. Jeanne Carmine told me that Marilyn called her at 10:00 pm that night, asking her to come over. Claiming exhaustion, Carmine declined but noticed something "strange" in Marilyn's voice.

Marilyn was alive when Kennedy left the house. I know this because she wrote about the night events in her diary. So what else happened to Marilyn that night?

Did the Secret Service give her a lethal dose of sedative, as Bob believed?

What about Sam Giancana's three hitmen? Did they find their way into Marilyn's house and slip her a suppository. You can't eliminate the CIA and their hitman Robert Maheu either. Any government agency, including the United States Army, is not above suspicion, because of the sensitive information Marilyn could have known.

According to wiretaps, Peter Lawford arrived back at the house some point during the night, after Marilyn died. Fred Otash, one of the wiretappers, claimed Lawford was searching for the diary and love letters. It was here that the cover-up began as they tried to figure out how to report the death to the police and Coroner.

According to Lawford's ex-wife, he said that the Kennedys assured everyone that there would be no proper inquiry into her death. First, Lawford, the Doctors, and the housekeeper concocted a reasonable story so no real investigation would take place. Then they had to convince the police that this was a straightforward suicide and get the Coroner to release the body to a friendly mortuary that Fox studio had contacted. That turned out to be Westwood Mortuary. All was going well until, as Dr. Curphey put it, I got my hands on it.

After the attempt to remove Marilyn's body to an outside mortuary failed, deputies brought her remains to the Hall of Justice for a formal investigation. The Los

Angeles County Coroner did an excellent job of helping confuse the facts. There were at least two people at the autopsy, Dr. Noguchi and John Miner. I heard rumors as many as five were at the procedure but couldn't confirm these reports or identify who they were.

Dr. Curphey's toxicologist, Dr. Ralph Abernathy, found no poison in the blood when he first tested Marilyn's body. Later, he reported finding enough poison to kill five people, with no determination of how it got administered. He then destroyed her organs under orders from Dr. Curphey, preventing any future test from being made. According to County records, only two times in the history of Los Angeles was the liver, or any other tissue sample lost, Marilyn Monroe and Robert Kennedy. That is important to note.

The Suicide Investigation Team report determined in all probability Marilyn took her own life. There was some controversy about how she did it, but there was no effort made to solve this glaring mystery. Dr. Curphey impaneled two doctors that were supposed to make a thorough investigation. Still, all of their conclusions were based on statements from Marilyn's doctors and published news accounts.

No report ever made to the Coroner's Medical Department identified who prescribed the many medication containers found at the scene. Dr. Engelberg told the Coroner and the police that he had prescribed the Nembutal tablets found in Marilyn's throat along with other medications. However, none of those other medications appeared in Marilyn's system or those from the empty containers. Furthermore, no container or prescription materialized for the Chloral Hydrate.

According to Dr. Curphey and Suicide Team Investigators, Doctor Greenson testified how the death occurred and Marilyn's state of mind. However, only a week after her death, Dr. Greenson stated he never believed Marilyn's death was suicide. During an interview with Deputy District Attorney John Miner, the doctor expressed his genuine opinion and played audiotapes of Marilyn's most recent conversations to prove it.

The Los Angeles Police Department did a better job of hiding the facts. There were at least three separate reports by LAPD officers to determine how and when she died. High-level detectives were assigned to learn the facts surrounding her death. Yet almost none of their official reports or any dialog with the Coroner or Suicide Team remain in LAPD files.

Los Angeles Police Department Chief of Police, William Parker, supervised the official investigation. According to published reports, Parker assigned Captain James Hamilton to Marilyn's case. Hamilton handled the main investigation in an atmosphere of secrecy that excluded even his most trusted employees. He was a friend of Bobby Kennedy, having worked with him years earlier. According to Jay Margolis in his book, "Marilyn Monroe: A Case for Murder," Hamilton may have been a source of intelligence within the LAPD for Kennedy.

Public funds provide the Police, Coroner, and the District Attorney with a decent budget to investigate unusual deaths in the City and County of Los Angeles. For the most part, they do an excellent job under challenging situations. In this case, most likely, they were met with the highest power that Federal Agencies have over local municipalities, besides jurisdiction, "National Security." This classification is a way of protecting government interests and discouraging all local inquiries.

After apparently running into these kinds of complications, no official LAPD report arrived at the Coroner's Office containing all the facts. I may be getting a little ahead of myself because LAPD might have given documents to Dr. Curphey, and he chose to hide it. All I know is that in 1962, all official inquiries died suddenly.

After the official Corner's case was closed, a flood of information continued to arise, suggesting a cover-up. Marilyn Monroe's phone records from early August until her death went missing from the phone company. Bob Slatzer told me only two entities had enough power to seize phone records without a court order, J. Edgar Hoover of the FBI and the Kennedy Administration.

By 1993, my knowledge of Marilyn's case may have been second to only Bob Slatzer, who was my investigative partner. Our combined experiences had brought television and news media from around the world to hear us discuss the case. My participation with two District Attorney investigations and a short-lived grand jury probe has provided me insight into Marilyn's death, unlike any others. In the next few chapters, I will attempt to tie together all I have learned quickly.

In the 50 years following Marilyn Monroe's death, there has been intense speculation by many armchair sleuths and journalists as to whether Marilyn took her own life. All the participants have been named and sinister plots investigated, with every imaginable scenario being described despite the massive cover-up. To close this little piece of history, we'll look at some of the other significant investigations into Marilyn's death.

Internationally recognized private investigator and director of the Nick Harris Detective Agency, Milo Speriglio, wrote a book entitled *"Crypt 33: The Saga of Marilyn Monroe."* In this book, he accused President John Kennedy of ordering the hit. According to Speriglio, Monroe was the victim of a national security management hit by the CIA and the Mob.

He stated the motive to be Marilyn becoming a threat to the family. Calling the White House almost everyday, Marilyn became a hot topic among Washington insiders. After announcing a press conference with the threat of blowing the lid off her relationship with the brothers, she had become a security risk.

Speriglio describes how Johnny Roselli, known for his attempted assassination of Fidel Castro and allegedly Robert Kennedy, arrived at Marilyn's house with two associates. He says they overpowered her and forcefully administered a killer enema. His assertion was that Joe Kennedy, the President's father, hired Sam Giancana to kill Marilyn, and Giancana and Hoffa had set Bobby up for a scandal. However, the Kennedy cover-up worked when Peter Lawford sped Bobby away from the house and they avoided a family disaster.

Most of his conclusions were based on the tapes that Bernard Spindel and Fred Otash had recorded. I knew Milo and although we didn't get along, his research was respected. Bob once told me that Otash was offering his tapes to the highest bidder, so the possibility existed Milo heard the recordings. It would have been nice if District Attorney officials would have bought these tapes and made them public, but just like everything else, they probably would have simply disappeared forever.

The rectal insertion was my hot choice for cause of death, because of the lack of barbiturates in her stomach. When Doctor Abernathy, the County Toxicologist, destroyed the organs, it prevented any further test for a suppository. Marilyn wrote in her diary about the CIA providing Roselli with a pill or poison to kill Castro, so maybe Milo was on the right track.

"*Goddess*" author, Anthony Summers, television producer for the BBC, turned up evidence of the Robert Maheu and Howard Hughes, Monroe film in his investigation. His CIA disclosures verified Marilyn's description of being approached by Jim O'Connell and Maheu with a plan to discredit the Indonesian President.

Summers wrote that Marilyn did not intentionally kill herself, and left open the possibility of murder. His research indicated that Bobby Kennedy was in the house that night and found Marilyn already drugged. He then called an ambulance to take her to the hospital, but she died. Evidence of him being at the house was destroyed by Peter Lawford to avoid his association with the death.

In a later revelation, Summers quoted an unnamed source, who claimed to have heard tapes of Marilyn's final night. The source said Bobby and Marilyn were screaming at each other while Peter Lawford was trying to calm them down. At one point, according to the informant, there were sounds of a struggle, and Robert Kennedy may have pushed Marilyn onto the bed. He also said the tapes sounded like they were edited. The tapes, according to Summers, left the impression that Marilyn was dead when Bobby left the house.

Writing about the assassination of John F. Kennedy, he rejected the findings of the Warren Commission, and claimed that Kennedy was killed by a right-wing conspiracy, possibly including major organized crime figures, such as Johnny Roselli, Carlos Marcello, Santo

Trafficante, and Sam Giancana. Other figures possibly involved included David Ferrie, Gerry Patrick Hemming, Guy Banister, and E. Howard Hunt.

I have to give Summers credit for his persistence in finding out what happened to Marilyn Monroe. At first, we disagreed on what happened in the Coroner's Office, but he was the first to uncover CIA documents that confirmed what was in her diary. The disclosures stated that Marilyn had worked with the CIA to discredit a foreign diplomat, something I had told County Officials many years earlier.

In the book entitled "*Double Cross,*" written by Sam & Chuck Giancana, nephew and brother of Sam Giancana respectively, it is stated that Marilyn's killers listened to wiretaps and waited for an opportune time to strike. When the hit men overheard the argument between Marilyn and Bobby, it provided an opportunity to execute their murder; Kennedy had ordered Marilyn sedated, and left the house. Later, the assassins sneaked into her bedroom and gave her a lethal suppository.

This book supported the theory that Sam Giancana and the Mafia were involved in the murder. Marilyn said she first saw Giancana in New York at a meeting with the CIA. Fast forward to the ill-fated weekend party that Frank Sinatra gave, this is where the mob decided to make their move. Hoffa would provide the wire tapers and Giancana the muscle.

Was Marilyn really murdered this way? I'm not sure. What I can say is that what happened during those recording sessions with Bernard Spindel and Fred Otash made a lot of people think that Sam Giancana had the Hollywood actress killed.

"*The Last Days of Marilyn Monroe*" by Donald Wolfe is based on interviews that reveal much of the same information that I have. Wolfe adds his own extensive inquiry to those of several other journalists, based on interviews that have revealed a more candid telling with the passage of time.

His evidence seems clear and convincing that there was a murder. By the time of her death, Marilyn Monroe was so enmeshed in sex, highest-level politics, the Mafia, and concerns over national security that her life was in the gravest danger.

In his investigation, he discovered that she had maintained a long-standing sexual relationship with both John F. Kennedy and Robert Kennedy, and had a diary that included the content of many sensitive conversations with them concerning things like Castro and the Mafia. His chronicles of her final days names the killer, documents the mode of death, and identifies those who orchestrated the cover-up.

Donald Wolfe, who was an acquaintance of Marilyn's and a long-time screenwriter, investigated the facts surrounding Marilyn's death. His indignation that the death processing was not followed accordingly with proper legal procedures, such as a coroner's inquest and a grand jury investigation, were the same as mine.

My investigative partner and good friend, Robert Slatzer was a screenwriter and author. He published two books on Marilyn, *"The Life and Curious Death of Marilyn Monroe"* in 1974 and *"The Marilyn Files"* in 1993. Bob, who shared a very special relationship with Marilyn, was a leading authority on the subject and was among the first researchers to proclaim that she did not commit suicide.

From my point of view, Robert Slatzer assembled the largest body of evidence on Marilyn's death, including gathering officials from the Coroner's Office, District Attorney's Office, and Los Angeles Police Department, whom all proclaimed suicide was not the cause.

Bob was the first journalist to uncover the infamous wiretap recordings and make the public aware of their existence. The most significant evidence of a crime stems from these audiotapes, which Jimmy Hoffa had recorded. Bob heard some of these tapes and told me there was no telling how many different edited versions there were in existence.

Bob believed that Marilyn's diary was the motive for her murder, and the wire-tapping's had provided him the proof. He heard those recordings and was hopeful that one day they would resurface. Bob's exhaustive investigation into Marilyn's death has uncovered many other details, which never may have been exposed without his research.

From my perspective, the wiretaps and Marilyn's diary provided all the evidence needed to discount the suicide theory. Johnny Roselli and Sam Giancana said that the CIA had provided them with every imaginable kind of pill to kill someone. Many of which were not detectable with normal tests. All of this, combined with my experiences at the Coroner's Office, leaves very little doubt about her death.

This suicide thing had bothered me from the start. If you have been following the evidence, then one could make an argument that she had gotten in a little over her head, and decided to end it all, or had accidentally taken too many pills while trying to go to sleep. However, the facts do not lead to these conclusions, and all of this is not just another conspiracy theory.

I go back to the first report that came out of the toxicology lab. Thirty Nembutal tablets lodged in the throat and no trace of anything that could have killed her in the stomach or blood. This was the first evidence that should have raised a red flag. There wasn't even a trace of any other prescribed medications that she was supposed to be legitimately taking. Even with all those prescription bottles sitting on her bedside nightstand, none were present inside her system.

The death certificate stated 'Acute Barbiturate Poisoning' due to 'Ingestion of Overdose'. A final copy of the toxicology report revealed '4.5 milligrams percent' of Barbiturates in the blood and '8.0 milligrams percent' of Chloral Hydrate. Where did this poison come from?

Dr. Engelberg stated he had prescribed the Nembutal capsules that Dr. Noguchi said killed her. No one came forward with a prescription for Chloral hydrate. This is a sedative used in the short-term treatment of insomnia and induces sleep before surgery. It comes as a capsule and liquid form, either orally ingested or utilized as a suppository to insert rectally.

Since numerous capsules and containers of prescription drugs were found at the scene, all orally taken, it is difficult to conceive that some trace of these drugs would not be found in the stomach or intestinal tract. Since there are no findings of these drugs in the stomach, and knowing the results of the toxicology, one must seriously consider the possibility of an injection or the use of a suppository to account for the toxicology findings.

The question of the Nembutal is still a mystery. How did these pills get in her throat, and did they kill her? There are 3 possibilities:

1. She failed in her attempt to commit suicide when they lodged in her throat.
2. She took them to go to sleep or for pain either on purpose or accidentally.
3. Someone crammed them in her mouth to make it look like suicide.

No answers would have been forthcoming if the body had been taken to Westwood mortuary. The Coroner's Office would have assigned a Deputy Coroner to go to the mortuary and evaluate the case. Our doctor may or may not have decided to perform an autopsy. He could have chose to go along with the police assessment of the facts and just take blood samples. Fox Studio, who had called the mortuary, could have influenced this decision.

Either way, this would have added an extra day to the process, allowing the capsules to dissolve into the bloodstream before they could be discovered in the throat. No doubt that when I called for the body to be brought downtown, this forced a change of plans.

What this case always needed was someone to supervise the investigation and guarantee that the facts would be known. However, with the District Attorney's Office involved in the initial cover-up, all outside attempts to investigate her death have been thwarted in ways that can only make you scratch your head. Even the Los Angeles County Grand Jury could not penetrate the web of deceit and cover-up surrounding this case.

Future journalist and researchers must continue trying to solve the mystery surrounding Marilyn's death. Their writings are the impetus that keeps this story alive and provides the best opportunity for a new investigation to uncover the truth. The only advice I would offer is to begin with the U.S. Government and it's Intelligence agencies.

CHAPTER 14:
The FBI, CIA, and Mafia

Marilyn's involvement with U.S. Intelligence and Organized Crime is perhaps the most curious aspect of this investigation. Her association with these entities seems almost impossible to conceive. Still, the weight of evidence, which includes FBI and CIA disclosures, is indisputable.

Marilyn's own words may have offered the best description of her situation. The activities detailed in her diary reflected a woman trapped in a world with no escape. The public knew her Hollywood image, but beneath it was a complicated reality involving matters shaping the future of America. Once Marilyn got in, there was no getting out, and even her Hollywood fame couldn't save her. She was a little fish in a big pond, and we all know how that story ended.

Let's take a more in-depth examination of roles played by the FBI, CIA, and Mafia in Marilyn Monroe's death.

The Federal Bureau of Investigations is the nation's oldest and most prestigious intelligence agency. For many years, they were America's protectors, and the public loved them.   J. Edgar Hoover was the top watchdog and wielded power to do whatever deemed necessary for preserving public security. However, there was a fine line between security and violating the constitution. At some point, Hoover began to cross it.

A prime illustration was the Bureau illegally spying on members of the civil rights movement. The treatment of Martin Luther King Jr. and actress Jean Seberg are two cited examples.

Hoover directed the FBI to track King in 1957 and concluded that King was dangerous due to communist infiltration. After accusing one of King's most trusted advisers of working as an agent of communist influence over the movement, he placed wiretaps on King's home and office phones and bugged King's rooms in hotels as he traveled across the country. King was the victim of FBI leaks of unverified information to his bank, insurance company, and organization. The agency even sent taped conversations with other women to his wife. More than one FBI agent was at the scene in Memphis, at the time of King's assassination.

Seberg, an actress from Iowa, was also targeted by Hoover. He leaked false stories, claiming she was pregnant by a member of the Black Panther Party, whose cause she supported. The backlash of this smear campaign caused Seberg a series of nervous breakdowns that eventually killed her. The police report stated that she massively overdosed on barbiturates, and was ruled a "probable suicide" by the French coroner.

J. Edgar Hoover's tactics for protecting America from the so-called Communist threat knew no bounds. When Arthur Miller's name landed on his list, he cataloged every person Miller associated with. Marilyn's name surfaced at that time. She was recruited to retrieve information on Arthur Miller, detailing his Communist activities.

The FBI connection with Marilyn Monroe began from that moment and ended with bugging her house for the final six months of her life. Evidence suggests that FBI Director Hoover had shown his interest in her activities for many years. He reportedly spent hundreds of hours listening to tapes taken from every room in her house, or any place she stayed. We can assume that the Federal Bureau of Investigation was well aware of Marilyn's involvement with White House affairs, and knew from taped conversations that she had begun documenting her activities. Hoover was concerned that anything Monroe passed on about the President or U.S. Intelligence would pose a tremendous threat to National Security.

When Marilyn went to Mexico City in 1962, she had meetings with assembled communist activists. FBI and CIA disclosures have also placed Lee Harvey Oswald there that same year. Is it possible that Marilyn Monroe attended a meeting with Oswald in 1962? Little more than a year before he allegedly assassinated President Kennedy? We know that after her trip, the FBI director in Mexico City sent a memo to Hoover about Marilyn attending the "Fair Play For Cuba" meetings.

The FBI's primary focus seemed to be with domestic communist activities. Government documents indicate they were very much aware of Marilyn being in Mexico City in 1962. FBI officials in Mexico filed a report on visits to the Soviet and Cuban embassies. According to J. Edgar Hoover's secretary, two weeks after this report reached FBI headquarters, Hoover talked to President Kennedy about her involvement with the Cubans.

At least in part, his purpose was not only warning Kennedy about the national security implications but also to rub the President's womanizing in his face. Nothing in the available record shows what was discussed at that meeting, or if Hoover mentioned Monroe's involvement with the FBI or CIA endeavors. Once you start to include international issues into this conversation, it broadens the scope of people who could have serious concerns.

Let's get this straight; the closest the world has come to nuclear war was the Cuban Missile Crisis of October 1962, which was only two months after Marilyn died. Fidel Castro, afraid of an assassination by the CIA and an invasion by the United States, had negotiated with the Soviet Union to install nuclear missiles to protect Cuba. The planning and construction of those weapons coincided with the "Fair Play For Cuba" meetings.

It's hard to believe they didn't discuss the possibility of this kind of activity at the White House. Marilyn was at the CIA meetings, where the threat of Castro was talked about. She was in Mexico City with the Fair Play for Cuba Committee when the missile bases were arming.

The Cuban populace easily noticed the arrival and deployment of the missiles, and hundreds of reports reached U.S. Intelligence. Countless sightings of large trucks traveling through towns were discussed in the circles Marilyn was traveling in. These trucks were reportedly carrying the launchers to the bases.

Finally, we don't know what Marilyn learned about the Cuban missiles or any other clandestine activities, but we know that Hoover began wiretapping Marilyn's home and was informed about all calls received and dialed in her house regarding any potential national security matters.

With the Cuban missile situation in the deployment stage and CIA directing secret missions in Cuba, anything Marilyn said on the subject, in her house, or on her phone, would have been of interest to the Cubans, Soviets, and for that matter the rest of the world.

The Bureau wanted to know everything about Marilyn, the CIA, the Kennedys, and all national security issues discussed. They monitored her activities around the clock, so it stands to reason that Hoover knew key details about her death. The question we have to ask is why withhold this information from the public. Did J. Edgar Hoover and the Federal Bureau of

Investigation consider Marilyn's death a matter of national security?

When the wiretaps revealed that Marilyn had written notes on Bobby Kennedy's conversations and details about some CIA meetings, they probably went on high alert. The FBI always fought an all-out war against crime, subversion, and communism. So their presence kind of makes sense, considering the history between Marilyn and them.

Marilyn's fate will always link to the FBI and Robert Maheu, in my opinion. From first contact, they formed a relationship that may have been more strategic than even her relationships with the Kennedys. Perhaps someday, the Bureau will release more information on their interactions before and after Arthur Miller. Somehow I believe that Monroe and Maheu had ties deeper than we may ever know.

Now let's examine her circumstances with the CIA. The first time Marilyn mentioned the Central Intelligence Agency is when she met Jim O'Connell. In her diary, this occurred at a meeting in New York with President John Kennedy and his advisors. She called him Big Jim of the Spy Boys. O'Connell, at that time, was Coordinator of the Assassination Plots against Castro for the CIA.

According to the diary and Senate Hearing disclosures, Marilyn Monroe was meeting with John Kennedy, then President of the United States; Jim O'Connell, Central Intelligence Agency Coordinator;

Robert Maheu, FBI, and CIA operative; and Mafia members Sam Giancana and Johnny Roselli, all discussing illegal things like killing somebody.

Marilyn's work for the Central Intelligence Agency didn't end there. In 1962, Jim O'Connell transferred to Asia, where he became Chief Regional Security Officer for the Far East. This job included numerous attempts to undermine foreign governments or assassinate their leaders. Marilyn would make entries in her diary about working with O'Connell and Robert Maheu, planning the overthrow of a government. CIA disclosures have confirmed her description of those meetings and the events she wrote about in her diary.

After Marilyn met John Kennedy, he became President of the United States. Shortly after that, as described in her diary, she began attending high-level intelligence meetings. This chain of events leaves little doubt that Marilyn was well on her way to becoming an agent for the United States Government.

CIA operatives are certainly not above suspicion in Marilyn's death. Surely after hearing about how unstable her home life had become, they worried about her knowledge of agency affairs. According to its own disclosures, Central Intelligence participated in the assassination of World Leaders from its inception. Still, there wasn't a lot of information on their activities concerning the matter. The agency was able to restrict newspapers from reporting about certain events. For example, the CIA's plots to overthrow Iran's governments in 1953 and Guatemala in 1954 were not reported by most news organizations.

Even before the Bay of Pigs, CIA minds were strategizing to keep Cuba out of Communist hands. Their attempt to use the Mafia to help overthrow Castro began during the Eisenhower administration. This meant that O'Connell's plot to kill the Cuban leader started before John Kennedy took office. Of course, this was illegal, not that the Mafia cared, but the House Select Committee on Assassinations did call the CIA into question. Under sworn testimony, Big Jim O'Connell answered these questions from the committee:

Question: (Committee) When did this operation begin? In other words, when did you first meet with Roselli?

Answer: (O'Connell) That would have been September of 1960.

Question: (Committee) And who was present during this conversation? This is the one at the Plaza Hotel in New York.

Answer: (O'Connell) Maheu, Roselli, and myself.

Question: (Committee) Did there come a time when other individuals were brought into the project?

Answer: (O'Connell) At this point in time, no.

Question: (Committee) When, in fact, did other individuals become involved in the operation?

Answer: (O'Connell) Well, after Mr. Roselli rather reluctantly agreed to participate in this type of operation, he brought in other individuals who I knew only by pseudonyms, "Sam Gold" and "Joe One Joe."

Question: (Committee) When these individuals were identified using these names, had you met them personally?

Answer: (O'Connell) No.

Question: (Committee) When did you first learn their true identities? The identities of Sam Gold and Joe.

Answer: (O'Connell) In the Sunday paper, there was an article, identifying the leaders of the Mafia. In that article, there were pictures of Sam Gold, who was identified as Momo Giancana and Joe, was identified as Santos Trafficante. And Mr. Maheu claimed this was the first time he was aware of just who we were dealing with.

Question: (Committee) Alright, what did you do upon learning that the individuals involved in this operation were in fact organized crime leaders?

Answer: (O'Connell) I contacted Colonel Edwards and told him what we had discovered, or at least, as far as I was concerned, it was the first indication I had who we were dealing with, and appraised them of his identities.

Question: (Committee) And what did he say to you? What instructions did he give you, if any?

Answer: (O'Connell) Well, he just said, well, this is probably what we could have expected, I suppose. And I don't want to be quoting him, because I don't recall really what he said, but apparently, he did not feel we should alter our approach to the assignment.

Question: (Committee) Did he give you any further instructions -- any additional instructions -- upon learning the identities of these persons?

Answer: (O'Connell) No. As I recall we just proceeded.

These meetings took place prior to John Kennedy's election, headed up by Vice President Richard Nixon. After Kennedy became President, he took charge of the plot and participated in these planning sessions with the assassins. When I read Marilyn's account of some of the meetings with these people in 1962, it didn't have the same meaning that it does now. There was more information in that book, but I didn't have the time or inclination to digest it.

Bits and pieces of information have been released through the Freedom Of Information Act, which has made me more knowledgeable about the importance of the contents. The FBI and CIA documents, and what other researchers were uncovering, brought her words to life. This has been a slow process, but the scenario that many denied is coming into full view. At first, everyone thought I was crazy, but time has proved Lionel Grandison to be correct.

A CIA document appeared sometime in the early 1990s, regarding the transcripts of wiretaps on Marilyn's house. A researcher had gone to the CIA's Agency Release Panel with a request, under the Freedom of

Information Act; to release existing documents in their possession regarding government wiretaps on Marilyn Monroe's telephones.

A documented CIA report written August 3, 1962, only a day before Marilyn Monroe's death show high government officials were in a state of extreme anxiety. The Kennedy brothers had been imparting sensitive information to Marilyn, and she was writing a lot of it down in her little red "diary of secrets."

CIA wiretaps of conversations between Marilyn Monroe and Robert Kennedy revealed some interesting points. The report contained these statements:

1.   Subject repeatedly called the Attorney General and complained about the way she was being ignored by the President and his brother.

2.   Subject threatened to hold a press conference and would tell all.

3.   Subject made reference to "bases" in Cuba and knew of the President's plan to kill Castro.

4.   Subject made reference to her "diary of secrets" and what the newspapers would do with such disclosures.

A part of the report is blacked out for National Security reasons. The document is signed by James Angleton, who was the Chief of Counterintelligence for the CIA.

During the early sixties, the Nuclear Arms Race was in full effect. Russia and the United States were playing a dangerous game of chicken by testing nuclear weapons at an alarming rate. On July 17, 1962, Robert Kennedy, with presidential adviser, General Maxwell D. Taylor at his side, witnessed one of these nuclear tests. Code-named "Little Feller," Kennedy was fully briefed on U.S. Military nuclear capabilities. Any widespread discussion would have brought United States Military Intelligence into the picture.

The CIA's bugging of Marilyn's house has profound implications. They were monitoring all conversations Bobby would have had with the White House or any other individuals discussing sensitive security issues. Most importantly, CIA operatives heard everything happening before, during, and after Marilyn's death. They knew what transpired that night and how the investigation progressed during the day. The agency knew every detail about Marilyn Monroe, and when they left didn't even bother to take their equipment.

After reading the disclosure, I wished that the grand jury could have seen the same document. Maybe that would have turned the tides and forced the District Attorney's Office to continue their so-called threshold Inquiry until they got it right. If they just could have determined what killed her, then we would have been a step closer.

Although they could not find her diary, they knew it had been in the Coroner's Office. It was apparent that the Coroner had been forced to cover up the cause of death. Maybe the CIA or the FBI had asked them to help conceal what happened, just as they did with the

Los Angeles Police Department. The District Attorney was plausibly in a no-win situation.

The significance of the wiretap disclosure has to do with the fact that Monroe was murdered the following day. The suggestion that somehow the CIA was involved in a domestic murder of an American citizen is not too far-fetched. Especially when considering past abuses from the agency's Counter Intelligence program, with its "absolute security at any cost" philosophy.

Whether or not the CIA authorized the hit is unknown. However, the way her body was found and moved around; the fashion in which reports were changed to reflect suicide; and the theft of her secret diary less than 48 hours after it arrived at the Coroner's Office; all have similarities to covert CIA methods used to conceal the truth.

In 1960, Retired US Army Colonel Truman Smith, writing in *Reader's Digest* about the KGB, who were the Soviet's version of the CIA, declared:

"It is difficult for most of us to appreciate its menace, as its methods are so debased as to be all but beyond the comprehension of any normal person with a sense of right and wrong."

One of the KGB methods that the good colonel found so despicable was making sex films used as blackmail. He wrote,

"People depraved enough to employ such methods, find nothing distasteful in more violent methods."

We would like to think that our own Intelligence Agency would heed this set of values. Yet, as we found out in Iraq, no rules are observed when it comes to protecting America. During the time of Colonel Smith's statement, Jim O'Connell began to use Marilyn to devise his own plan. After seeing her at the Castro plot meetings, he thought her perfect for his plans in the Far East.

I assume O'Connell's superiors at the CIA knew about President Kennedy bringing Marilyn into meetings where Agency business was getting discussed. However, we have to look at how a CIA Officer would get placed in the position of conversing his plans in a room with Marilyn because it calls into question her security clearance.

Once again, I ask, why would John Kennedy bring Marilyn to these meetings? Did he know something about Marilyn nobody else knew? One thing is certain, the CIA and the FBI both developed a relationship with Marilyn Monroe. Undoubtedly, it was in their best interest to know what she was doing.

The CIA's charter bans domestic spying, but in 1976, the final report of the special Senate subcommittee, headed by Idaho Senator Frank Church, to investigate CIA abuses, concluded that the Agency had amassed files on more than 7,000 American citizens and 1,000 domestic organizations. That information was disseminated in thousands of reports to the FBI and other agencies.

Marilyn's house was bugged from February until the day she died. Any calls Robert Kennedy made to or from her home were being recorded. Spy games were running amok in Marilyn's world, and looking back now, the final ending was predictable.

As early as 1963, the FBI and CIA knew of the Spindel and Otash electronic surveillance of Marilyn's house. The authorities must have heard from their sources that tapes were circulating, so they arrested Otash in an attempt to seize them. Their investigation into the John F. Kennedy assassination led them to believe that Otash had uncovered some link between Marilyn and the murder. It is a known fact that the FBI had its own recordings but found out that the Mafia and Jimmy Hoffa also had a copy.

Sam Giancana's assorted ties to John Kennedy have long been the theme of speculation. In 1960, Giancana was believed to have assisted in John F. Kennedy's Presidential election in Illinois. It appears the Chicago Mob boss had good reason to feel betrayed by the Kennedy Administration. The Attorney General was putting enormous legal pressure on Organized Crime.

However, the two had a nemesis in common, Fidel Castro. Mob leaders, who wanted to exploit Cuba's endless gambling potentials, hated Castro ever since he started governing it. The US Government deemed his communist system of government, a hazard to national security, as evidenced by the Bay of Pigs invasion in April 1961. Marilyn's writings put US Government officials and Mob leaders in the same room, discussing how to get rid of this nemesis.

Giancana's personality had rubbed many people in the wrong way, possibly including Kennedy. Known as the man who orchestrated the infamous Valentine's Day Massacre, he was a ruthless assassin who rose to power by killing those who got in his way. He was assassinated himself in 1975, in the basement of his Illinois home in Oak Park; some suspected it was a hit by government agents.

Giancana was killed shortly before he was scheduled to appear before a U. S. Senate committee investigating an ostensible CIA and Mafia collusion in plots to assassinate President John F. Kennedy. Some commentators have alleged that the CIA killed Giancana because of his troubled history with the agency.

Another theory is that a New York crime family ordered Giancana's murder, due to fears that he would testify about Mafia. The other hitman, Johnny Roselli, who Marilyn wrote was involved in the CIA plots to kill Fidel Castro, was found stuffed in an oil drum floating off the coast of Miami. Remember the DA's investigator, Frank Hronek, who suspected the mafia? He uncovered evidence that Marilyn was murdered to keep her silent. This was the only public statement made by a government investigator, claiming another possible scenario to Marilyn's death. The evidence revealed is substantial, pointing to this conclusion, although there remain several conflicting stories as to what role the Mafia played that Saturday night in August.

The most condemning information we were able to obtain was from the wire-tapers and Sam Giancana's relatives, who wrote a book. How can your most incriminating evidence come from organized crime figures, and not from our own Law Enforcement agencies?

After Marilyn attended Frank Sinatra's party the weekend before her death, she wrote about drinking and talking too much. By all accounts, her conversations led Sam Giancana, the Al Capone of the sixties, to think he had major problems with Monroe's state of mind. During the party, she boasted about revealing the contents of her diary, which disclosed information regarding him working as an operative for the CIA.

This disclosure would cause serious concerns within his organization, and he hoped to hide it from other Mafia families. He had to make a move to protect his creditability. When Jimmy Hoffa told him he was going to bug her house, he saw a perfect opportunity to silence Marilyn. The wire tapers said that they were afraid of the mobsters that Giancana sent because they seemed more interested in killing Marilyn than anything else.

Bob said the most condemning part of the tapes was the interchange between Robert Kennedy and Marilyn as they were arguing about the whereabouts of the diary. After listening to the recordings, he asked did the wiretappers hear the murder being committed. They looked at each other and replied they didn't know, but he sensed certain uneasiness.

When the housekeeper found Marilyn unconscious, the wire tapers said they packed up and went home. If the death of Marilyn Monroe was recorded, the truth might only be revealed when and if one of these sets of tapes resurfaces. They could answer critical questions about how Marilyn actually died, and provide clues about who killed her.

Researchers, writers, and law enforcement officials who claim to have heard some of these tapes or were told what was on them have no doubt Marilyn was murdered. However, they can only speculate as to who did it. Most of the theories involve the mobsters from the wiretaps, Robert Kennedy, Secret Service, or Johnny Roselli with J. Edgar Hoover watching and listening.

Surprisingly not one of these audiotapes has ever been made public. Obviously, the CIA and FBI wiretaps were classified as national security matters, but the mafia tapes were different. What happened to those recordings? We can assume that Hoffa got a copy of all the tapes because he paid for the endeavor. Spindel and Otash each got their own because they were able to duplicate them. I believe the very intimidating Giancana got one as well. However, many other copies were made from these masters. We know they were edited due to the number of hours recorded. Where are they now?

It is evident that Hoffa used his tape to blackmail someone in the Justice Department because Robert

Kennedy decided to stop his investigation into the government's charges against Hoffa. After the murder of his brother, he didn't have the same interest or power. It was not until he resigned as Attorney General and started his bid for a seat in the United States Senate that the Hoffa conviction was realized.

Many people who were involved in this investigation have died. John and Robert Kennedy were murdered in front of numerous witnesses. Sam Giancana was murdered in his kitchen. While in jail, Bernard Spindel died mysteriously, and Jimmy Hoffa simply disappeared and rumored to have been buried under a stadium. At least Marilyn died in her bedroom, but are we to assume these events were all a coincidence?

> Marilyn dies in 1962...
> John Kennedy was murdered in 1963...
> Robert Kennedy was murdered in 1968...
> Bernard Spindel died in 1968...
> Jimmy Hoffa disappeared in 1974...
> Sam Giancana was killed in 1975...

Spindel died while serving time for illegally tapping the phone of a prominent New York attorney. The cause of death was reported to be a heart attack at the age of forty-five. According to his wife, it was a consequence of prison officials failing to give him his medicine.

New York County (Manhattan) District Attorney Frank S. Hogan confiscated Spindel's tapes and files at his home. Now get this, Bernard bugged his own house. When the detectives served the subpoena, he activated the recorder and taped them saying, "Find the Marilyn files."

Mrs. Spindel once claimed she had positive proof from taped conversations amongst the police, who talked about the Marilyn Monroe connection while at her house. Her husband's files on Monroe and Bobby Kennedy were amongst the things they were looking for.

December 21, 1966, the New York Times ran a three-column story by Robert Tomasson.

Tomasson wrote:

"In an affidavit submitted to the court, Bernard Spindel had filed suit for the return of bugging devices and tapes of Marilyn Monroe. He asserted that some of the material contained tapes and evidence containing the circumstances surrounding the cause of death of Marilyn Monroe."

The New York District of Attorney's Office responded by saying the evidence was lost. But they didn't know Spindel. He not only had copies stashed all over New York, but had tapes of the raid on his house that showed the FBI was involved.

In 1992, the Los Angeles Times ran a story written by Myrna Oliver, a Times Staff Writer. She wrote in part:

Fred Otash: Colorful Hollywood Private Eye and Author

"Fred Otash, legendary Hollywood vice cop and private eye has died at the age of 70. The colorful Otash, who had just completed a book titled "*Marilyn, Kennedy, and Me*" about the death of Marilyn Monroe, died Monday in his West Hollywood home of natural causes. Otash is rumored to have been one of the investigators who kept a physical and electronic surveillance on Marilyn Monroe in the months before her death."

In 1976 his book, "*Investigation Hollywood: Memoirs Of Hollywood's Top Private Detective,*" was published. Otash claimed in this book that after President Kennedy was assassinated, the FBI confiscated files he maintained on Kennedy. In 1963, he was arrested for not revealing who else was involved in the conspiracy to kill Marilyn and Kennedy.

I often wondered why Albert Stiller made a point of saying the Secret Service wanted to talk to me. Although they never approached me, just the mention of them was cause for concern. Deputy Lester Goldberg had spoken to them, Milo had pointed a finger at them in his book, and Bob had accused them of the murder.

One would figure that the two agents who came to the Coroner's Office were Kennedy's men, looking for the journal that Marilyn was supposed to have. The agency was said to be a wing of White House security, but probably owed some of their allegiance to the U.S. Army that trained them. United States Army Intelligence had a significant stake in this game because of the nuclear weapons issue in Cuba.

A short time after Marilyn died, John Kennedy would face one of his biggest challenges. He woke up one morning and found tactical nuclear weapons ninety miles off the United States coast. The Soviet field commanders who operated the missiles were authorized to use them if the United States invaded Cuba. The fate of millions hinged upon the President's ability to navigate the right course of action.

All of the available research suggests that the U.S. first obtained photographic evidence of the missiles in October when a CIA U-2 pilot captured images of what were identified as medium-range ballistic missiles. When the President was briefed on the CIA's analysis of the photos, Kennedy chose to use a U.S. Naval quarantine of foreign ships carrying offensive weapons for Cuba, as opposed to a blockade of all materials heading for their ports. A classic blockade could not be used, because it would have to take place in international waters.

The Soviets responded to the quarantine by sending 14 ships, presumably carrying weapons to Cuba. Kennedy issued a stern statement that he would send his nuclear-armed Navy to intercept the Soviet armada. The world held its breath as the two most powerful countries headed for their meeting in the Atlantic Ocean. Thank God the Soviets blinked and turned back to Russia, averting a possible calamity.

It was rumored that even on the brink of his meeting with destiny, Kennedy was occupied with his newest love.

When the CIA came to notify the President of the crisis, the Secret Service informed them that there was a 'Do Not Disturb' sign on his private room in the White

House. They advised them to take the report of nuclear weapons in Cuba to Secretary of State, Robert McNamara.

You can imagine what the Generals of the United States Army and the Admirals of the United States Navy thought about the leader the voters had sent them. The relationship had started badly with the Bay of Pigs. Although the planning wasn't his, it was still Kennedy's responsibility, as Commander-in-Chief, to finalize the operation. When the CIA was thrown out of Cuba, the Army wanted to invade and get their prestige back. They never forgave President Kennedy for opposing them.

The strong military complex that former President Dwight Eisenhower had warned Americans about was beginning to flex its muscles. Maybe the military wanted to take an active role in running the government. I remember when one of America's most gifted Generals, Alexander Haig, was chosen as Secretary of State. President Reagan was shot, and when the Vice President was unavailable, he brazenly stated,

"I've got everything under control," and America shuttered.

To the American public, Kennedy was a hero. His Administration had averted a nuclear war when the military complex wanted a confrontation. He was killed a few months later, after only a little more than two years in office. Not since Abraham Lincoln's assassination had America mourned so deeply for the death of a President. The political rock star was gone. Gone was Camelot. But his hope for America still lived.

CHAPTER 15:
The Usual Suspects

Life has a funny way of sweeping you in unimaginable directions. Who would have thought that Robert Slatzer and I would have crossed paths as we did in 1974, nearly twelve years after my Coroner's Office experience? Up until then, only the assassinations of John and Robert Kennedy offered any clues to her death. I honestly believed the case of Marilyn Monroe was completely dead and had made up my mind to stay out of that mass of confusion.

However, Bob's passion for bringing justice to Marilyn inspired me. His sincerity and dedication to this task were infectious. Nobody cared about Marilyn Monroe more than Robert Slatzer. He told me that he and Marilyn met at Fox Studio's lot when she was a model. On a weekend rendezvous in Ensenada, Mexico, where they married and returned to California. When Twentieth Century Fox discovered it, they undid the marriage by burning the certificate filed with the Mexican court.

A native of Marion, Ohio, Bob attended Ohio State University and began his writing career as a reporter for the Scripps Howard newspapers. He came to Hollywood in 1946 to write about the movie business. Eventually, Bob found work in films as a screenwriter, director, and producer. He wrote and directed several "B" movies. In addition, he wrote a book called "*Duke: The Life and Times of John Wayne*" and another called "*Bing Crosby: Hollow Man.*"

In 1974, Bob had written, and his publisher was releasing "*The Life and Curious Death of Marilyn Monroe.*" On the promotional tour for this very revealing book, he walked the studio where I produced a Public Affairs radio program. We struck up a friendship that lasted until he died in 2005. I talked to Bob after his surgery before he passed. He encouraged me to write a book to document what we had done over the last thirty years. He wanted me to sell the idea of a feature film to a studio.

He implored me to keep telling what happened in the Coroner's Office. Bob looked at me and said, "disclose everything you know about the case and diary because I know you haven't told it all." Even while laying in his hospital bed, Marilyn was always on his mind. He loved her until the very end.

Bob said he would try to live long enough to help me with the book and movie. Of course, this wasn't to be the case, Robert Slatzer passed away not long after that.

Marilyn's writings were the one thing we had in common over the years because we had both seen it. I always felt Bob was uncomfortable with her CIA and the FBI dealings. When Castro or Sukarno's name came up, he never had anything to say about them. Once I asked him if he thought Marilyn was a communist, he aggressively answered, "no way."

We never discussed any of the FBI entries regarding the House Un-American Committee. However, there was no doubt that Bob had benefited from the Congressional attack on European and Jewish writers. Bob had come to Hollywood as a red, white, and blue American from the Midwest. He landed some of the writing jobs left open because publishers and studios would not hire an accused communist.

His problems began when, according to him, he married Marilyn and came up against one of Fox Studios' potential moneymakers. He was never interested in the other side of her existence, but only who killed her and removing the negativity associated with the suicide aspect of her death. So the true realities of her life were not discussed and left to other journalists to investigate. I'm not a journalist, but have researched what was in the diary and have developed some compelling conclusions.

Information gathered since 1962 has convinced me that the secrets of Marilyn's life and death resided in that diary. At first, I viewed Marilyn's notes as newsworthy, but as the years went by, its importance became increasingly evident. I began to understand that Marilyn was writing about a policy that impacted the fabric of America.

From Marilyn's time with Arthur Miller, while working for the FBI to her escapades with the Kennedy brothers, she was in the middle of consequential political activities with far-reaching ramifications.

The diary detailed these periods of her life in a uniquely profound way. Marilyn's writings were more than just a personal journal; they provided a spellbinding glimpse into the high stakes world in which we all live.

Even as stories of sex parties began to appear, it never swayed my opinion of the social value of her writings. I never felt any inclination to connect America's enduring movie star and sex symbol to the murky world of international skullduggery. After all, her legacy has endured 50 years of controversy since her death, and she is still America's sweetheart. However, with that said, the significance of the information in her diary is undeniable.

Kennedy, the Secret Service Agents, and Peter Lawford had searched Marilyn's house looking for her diary. The CIA and FBI both had wiretaps, presumably looking for the same thing. Jimmy Hoffa and Sam Giancana sent wiretappers, and Mafia hitmen to find it. Without a doubt, if that diary had not disappeared from the Coroner's Office and been made public, its impact would have altered future events in ways unimaginable.

Over the years, the growing relevance of her journal has continued to amaze me. Maybe, if time had permitted, I would have read the whole book and found more revelations. However, someone with a key or combination to the Coroner's Office safe took it out of circulation. It has never shown up publicly again.

The architects of the Marilyn Monroe cover-up were active participants in her death right from the start. A good indication of that is the concocted story about that night and how shallow the official police investigation has been ever since.

It is hard to figure out what the Los Angeles Police Department knew because they never made the results public. Although they had some of their top detectives investigating her case, the only witnesses ever spoken to were Marilyn's doctors and housekeeper. Jack Clemmons once told me the Los Angeles Police Department's investigation of Marilyn's death was shameful. You could smell the stench of a cover-up all the way to the White House.

In 1993, Bob Slatzer and I went to Police Headquarters for an updated file regarding her case. They told us no official report on Marilyn's death existed. Why wouldn't there be a public file on Marilyn's death?

Constitutional law researchers have made the individual's rights a point of contention against the United States Government's interest in protecting an intelligence asset. In 2010, a new document, released under the Freedom of Information Act, verified the CIA was bugging Marilyn's house the night she died. But how does the Freedom of Information Act relate to local government in particular with Marilyn Monroe's death?

Marilyn's writings and my subsequent investigation have shown many complications that could have influenced the Los Angeles Police Department, LA County Coroner, and District Attorney investigations. Although some specifics remain unclear, the cast of characters participating in either the cover-up or death of Marilyn Monroe has become unmistakable.

Here's the list of usual suspects:

The Kennedy Family

Marilyn's relationship with the Kennedy's is the most plausible reason for her death. From her introduction to John in the late fifties until the night she died, Marilyn became entrenched in a world where there was no escape. Not for her, and ultimately not for John or Robert Kennedy either. These three, destined to die within six years of each other, each departed under shadowy circumstances.

Although her relationship with Bobby Kennedy seems more directly related to her death, it was John who placed her in harm's way by bringing her to CIA meetings with the Mafia. Why bring her to those meetings? Did Marilyn have a security clearance? Was she already a briefed and active member of the U.S. Intelligence Community? Whatever the answers, Marilyn would represent a security threat that sent the

Federal Bureau of Investigations and Central Intelligence Agency scurrying to wiretap her house and phones.

By all accounts, Marilyn was genuinely in love with Bobby Kennedy. She believed he was going to leave his wife to marry her. Her last days with Bobby were a sad commentary to their overall relationship. Marilyn's best friend, Jeanne Carmine, told me that Marilyn's affair with John Kennedy was all fun and games. They partied around town; everyone in the Industry knew about their relationship. However, with Bobby, it was much different. Carmine said Marilyn fell hard for him, and she remembers them "kissing madly" during the special moments they shared.

Another of Marilyn's good friends, Terry Moore, said Marilyn really believed Bobby loved her, and that one day he would become President of the United States, and she, his First Lady. Their relationship was secretive, but her friends were present many times when they were together.

Jeanne described being there when Bobby first discovered Marilyn was keeping a journal of her activities with him. She said Bobby had come over to Marilyn's place and found the diary lying on the table. She recalled him being livid and confronting Marilyn about the book. "What is this," he asked her. Marilyn related that it was her diary. She wanted to be able to remember things so she could talk to him later about it. Carmine said Kennedy told her, "Get rid of it. Get rid of it now!"

The night of Marilyn's death, Bobby Kennedy and Peter Lawford were at Marilyn's house according to multiple eyewitness accounts. According to her diary and wiretap recordings, a violent argument occurred between Marilyn and Bobby. What happened after the argument and fight is sketchy, but wiretap evidence suggests that secret service agents may have sedated Marilyn before leaving the premises.

After her mysterious death, the Kennedy family began to handle the cover-up of Bobby being at the house the night she died. They also sought to play down any reference to John Kennedy's relationship with Marilyn from 1958 through 1962. It was a masterful job by professionals with unlimited resources and the ability to reach almost anybody. They stonewalled every investigation by local law enforcement officials, and even after JFK's assassination, the cover-up continued.

With all that was known, the Kennedy connection was the logical place for investigators to start. But with White House denials, there were no facts to be found for their investigations. The Kennedy name made for great gossip and excited the public's imagination. Still, the reality was that no one could get any answers from them.

Let's develop one conspiracy theory from my experiences and research. I've mentioned that there are some links between the Kennedys' assassinations and Marilyn's death. There weren't enough ears to hear all the rumors, both real and imagined, but here's one that I've developed.

November 1960: Senator John F. Kennedy defeats Vice President Nixon in a close presidential election. Kennedy went ahead with the secret Nixon-Hunt plans for a CIA-backed invasion of Cuba. Howard Hunt was reportedly at Kennedy's side during the execution phase of the endeavor.

The invasion at the Bay of Pigs would be a monumental failure. CIA and Cuban exile leaders, such as Eugenio, blamed Kennedy for withholding planned military air cover. Kennedy threatens to dismantle the agency but opts to hire a new director instead. However, the friction from this incident would continue to simmer.

Meanwhile, Marilyn was also engaged in secret operations with the CIA. She makes a trip to Mexico City and attends a Fair Play For Cuba committee meeting. While there, Marilyn meets Lee Harvey Oswald, who is also working for the agency. She learns information that sends U.S. Intelligence operations into a mass frenzy.

Upon returning home, operatives have bugged her entire house. Conversations are recorded between her and Bobby Kennedy, discussing sensitive information. Also heard is Marilyn talking to members of the American Communist Party in Mexico City.

Joseph Kennedy, the family's patriarch, becomes aware of the threat Marilyn represents to his sons and the entire Kennedy family. Joe, who had made his fortune during the prohibition era, had genuine ties to organized crime. He gained some legitimacy when he was appointed ambassador to Great Britain. Still, even then, he was suspected of Nazi ties by the British.

There is evidence suggesting that Joe had taken out a contract with Sam Giancana to murder Marilyn.

After Giancana had fulfilled his contract, he expected the Kennedy Administration to ease their prosecution efforts against him, Jimmy Hoffa, and other organized crime members. That never happened.

The CIA and the Mafia would conspire to kill President Kennedy and use Lee Harvey Oswald as their fall guy. Oswald would then get brazenly murdered by one of Giancana's hitmen. We know that this would not have been the first time CIA operatives and mafia members worked together.

At the time, Robert Kennedy was powerless to do anything about his brother's murder. However, a few years later, he was on the verge of becoming President of the United States, which would have given him the power to expose the truth. That would have had far-reaching ramifications, shaking the very foundation of our nation. U.S. Intelligence could not allow that to happen, so Robert Kennedy was assassinated as well.

If ordered, Howard Hunt, Robert Maheu, and Jim O'Connell would not have hesitated to kill anybody. Giancana or Roselli would have done the same if paid. Marilyn and the Kennedy's lives were each intertwined, and all paid the price.

In the mid-90s, a collection of documents supposedly written by John Kennedy to Marilyn Monroe surfaced. These were known as the Cusack Papers, purportedly written by Kennedy in his own hand, discussing the relationship between Marilyn Monroe, Chicago gangster Sam Giancana and himself.

According to Lawrence Cusack, he found these documents in the attic of his deceased father's house. He states that his father died in 1985 after having served as a secret counselor to Kennedy. He claims that these correspondences were love letters and secret communications between the President and Marilyn Monroe.

The documents, later deemed to be forged, sold about 350 copies. In 1999, Cusack was found guilty of fraud and sentenced to ten years in prison. Many feel that Mr. Cusack's punishment was excessive and wrong. I am certainly one of those who understand that sentiment.

In 1962, Deputy Danbacker informed me about someone breaking into Marilyn's file cabinet. In 1974, Bob Slatzer told me about going to Marilyn's house days after her death and discovering the same. He also claimed Marilyn told him about some love letters she was keeping. The possibility exists that these Cusack Papers represent the missing documents taken from Marilyn's cabinet, and the Kennedy machine had managed to maintain the cover-up once again.

After his conviction, the Kennedy family sought to have these documents destroyed. They stated that there was a significant risk that the forgeries would re-enter the marketplace, and the only way to prevent this was to destroy them.

Many have spent considerable sums of money and want the documents returned, stating that they need appropriate testing. Others feel that even though they may be forgeries, they in themselves were a piece of history. I never heard the outcome of this case, but it proves the cover-up continues into the 21st century.

Peter Lawford

Peter Lawford was a British-born actor, who most people born after 1970 would never remember. Achieving acting fame as a child, Lawford appeared in numerous movies during the 1940s and 50s. He eventually became part of the famous "Rat Pack," including Frank Sinatra, Dean Martin, Sammy Davis Jr., and Joey Bishop. However, Lawford's biggest role didn't happen on the big screen but occurred in real life during his involvement with Marilyn Monroe and the Kennedys.

In 1954, Peter Lawford married Patricia Kennedy, sister of then U.S. Senator John Kennedy. At that time, Lawford was not a US citizen but had married into one of the country's most influential families. Lawford, along with Frank Sinatra, played huge roles in fundraising for JFK's presidential campaign. Eventually, Lawford would become the ultimate frontman for the entire Kennedy family. He became the protector of their family image and the Kennedy brothers' link to Hollywood glamour.

Lawford befriended Marilyn, and she spent considerable time at his home. In fact, she spent so much time there that J Edgar Hoover wiretapped Lawford's house, according to FBI disclosures. Entries in Marilyn's diary and wiretaps reveal he was fully aware of Marilyn's intentions to hold a press conference and pleaded with her to call it off.

There are conflicting stories about Lawford's whereabouts the evening Marilyn died, but according to her last diary entries and wiretap recordings, Lawford was at Marilyn's house that night. According to White House telephone logs, he called President Kennedy at 6:04 am on the morning of her death. No doubt, he was keeping the President abreast of the situation with Marilyn.

If anyone subscribes to the theory that Robert Kennedy had a role in Marilyn's death, then Peter Lawford would have been his chief conspirator. Many believe that Lawford handled the clean up at the crime scene while convincing both doctors and the housekeeper to lie to investigators in the interest of national security.

Amazingly, just a few years later, Peter Lawford's name was associated with another well-known celebrity, who died under more than mysterious circumstances. Dorothy Dandridge had been dating Lawford before her death. She was found dead at her home from an apparent self-administered drug overdose. A proclaimed suicide note was at the scene, but its authenticity questioned. However, there was no serious investigation ever performed. Dr. Theodore Curphey ruled her death an overdose from the anti-depressant drug Tofranil.

A subsequent examination would later show conflicting evidence as to how she died. As for Peter Lawford, who was still married to Patricia Kennedy at the time, his wife would file for a divorce less than a year after Dorothy Dandridge's death. Whether her death was accidental, suicidal, or something else remains a mystery to this very day.

Sam Giancana

Sam Giancana was a Sicilian American mobster and boss of the notorious "Chicago Outfit." During the 1950s, Giancana, along with other crime bosses, began setting their sights on building gambling casinos in Havana, Cuba. Hoping to make millions, these mobsters were negotiating with the Cuban President Fulgencio Batista, a U.S. friendly dictator.

Before their ambitious plans could materialize, a revolution began taking place in Cuba. This uprising, being fought by the country's peasants and farmers, was led by a man named Fidel Castro. Castro, being lauded as a champion of anti-imperialism, spearheaded the charge to ouster the system of inequality gripping their Caribbean Island.

The Central Intelligence Agency and the U.S. Government were also feeling the pinch of Castro's revolution. Many U.S. and European countries were heavily vested in Batista's presidency and wanted something done to prevent his overthrow. Big Jim O'Connell was appointed by CIA officials to head up a plot to kill Fidel Castro. O'Connell then turned to the intelligence communities' number one operative, Robert Maheu.

Based in Las Vegas, Maheu began orchestrating a plan that would ultimately lead to Sam Giancana's involvement with Marilyn Monroe. Being the smooth operative he was, Maheu put together an unprecedented plan to hire mobsters, who would assassinate Fidel Castro.

CIA documents reveal that Maheu was close associates with mobster hitman Johnny Roselli. He knew him as a Las Vegas bigwig who rolled with billionaire tycoon, Howard Hughes.

Maheu told Roselli about an international businessman willing to pay $150,000 for a Castro hit. Roselli then set up a meeting attended by Giancana, Roselli, Maheu, and Big Jim O'Connell. By most accounts, these mobsters would make subsequent attempts to assassinate the Cuban leader but were never successful.

When John Kennedy became President, Cuba was the nation's hottest crisis, and O'Connell needed to brief him on what the CIA had in mind for Castro. Kennedy anticipated a showdown with the Cuban leader and told

O'Connell to set up additional meetings with Giancana and Roselli.

Marilyn Monroe attended at least two of these meetings. Not only does she describe them in her diary, but CIA disclosures have confirmed these meetings took place as well. Sam Giancana was never happy about Kennedy bringing Marilyn to these meetings. That was a tenuous situation for him, working in cahoots with the U.S. Government. If the other crime families were to find out, they would not have been pleased. Marilyn was an unexpected wildcard that Giancana never saw coming.

Flash forward two years, and Giancana's worst fear was becoming a reality. Marilyn carelessly liked to dress up and go to Frank Sinatra's lavish parties; she shows up at one of these parties the weekend before she dies. While there, Marilyn gets drunk as hell and starts talking about holding a press conference to reveal everything about the Kennedys. Giancana became livid and decided he needed to do something about this pestilent situation quickly.

Union Boss Jimmy Hoffa also attended that Frank Sinatra party. He knew of Marilyn's connection with the Kennedys and wanted to use her for getting a foothold in the Justice Department. Together they would develop a plan to murder her and blame it on Bobby Kennedy.

The first part of the plan was to have Teamster President Jimmy Hoffa hire Bernard Spindel and Fred Otash to bug Marilyn's house. Hoffa's initial target was her diary, needing it for leverage. However, these wiretappers were unaware that the overall plan was to murder her.

The second part was to listen for the opportune moment, and then unleash Giancana's professional hitmen on Marilyn. If the plan had worked, Monroe would be dead, and Robert Kennedy blamed. Jimmy Hoffa would then have a shot at blackmailing the government into dropping the charges against him. Sam Giancana would have shut Marilyn up for good.

As U.S. Attorney General, Robert was actively trying to convict Hoffa for his shady union practices. He didn't know he had also become the target of a sinister plot to get rid of Marilyn and completely disgrace his own family.

Now the question remains, did Giancana contact Robert Maheu or Jim O'Connell to complain about Marilyn's threats? We know they were all plotting together to kill Castro with a suppository. We also know that the CIA and FBI had wiretap lines at Marilyn's home. Was Marilyn a big enough threat to warrant a decision to kill her by intelligence and mafia members? Indeed, the Central Intelligence Agency had the power to orchestrate a cover-up of this magnitude, and Sam Giancana had the resources to make sure nobody ever heard anything from Marilyn again.

As a footnote to this story, when Lee Harvey Oswald allegedly assassinated President Kennedy, he was gunned down before he could ever go to trial. The man who killed him, Jack Ruby, was employed by Sam Giancana.

A few years later, one of Giancana's relatives was quoted in the Los Angeles Times, saying he killed Marilyn with a suppository in the rectum. He later died in his jail cell. Why am I not surprised?

Robert Maheu

Robert Maheu may be the Keyser Söze of this whodunit. In fact, the only constant throughout this investigation has been Maheu. The more we examine his role, the more he appears to be the puppet master of this twisted tale. Remember, all of this began with Maheu, who was also known as "Iron Bob." He introduced himself to Marilyn as a Federal Bureau of Investigations agent who, as she put it, "wanted me to do something for America." Maheu would then ask Marilyn to gather information about the communist activities of Arthur Miller, promising her a lucrative film deal in return.

He first approached her in the early to mid-fifties, when she knew nothing about the Kennedys or the intelligence community. Marilyn was just another young, struggling Hollywood actress full of insecurities, seeking stardom and willing to do almost anything to achieve it.

Maheu already had his operation in place when he introduced himself to Marilyn. Paula Strasberg was part of the team, employed to cozy up to Marilyn. Maheu made sure their relationship got even more comfortable.

It was Strasberg who convinced Marilyn that working with him was the right thing to do. She taught Marilyn about the inner workings of communism, including the language, organization, and what information Maheu and the Federal Bureau of Investigations needed.

After Marilyn successfully allowed the government to bring charges against Arthur Miller, she got introduced to John F. Kennedy. You have to question the occurrence and timing of this introduction. Kennedy was a known playboy from his Harvard days, and it was like sending a lamb to the slaughter. The only question is, who really got slaughtered?

All available evidence suggests that Robert Maheu arranged to have Marilyn introduced to John Kennedy. Although called a close friend and confidant of the Kennedys, the facts point to something different. Maheu was a double agent who worked for both the FBI and CIA. Before the Kennedy presidency, he already had involvement with the revolution taking place in Cuba. The Central Intelligence Agency was concerned about whether the new administration would continue to support its clandestine efforts there.

Maheu's spy work brought him in contact with Howard Hughes. Hughes was the CIA's largest contractor and proclaimed richest man in the world. He was a renowned playboy and filmmaker who discovered movie goddesses Jane Russell and Jean Harlow. Hughes was once married to one of Marilyn's close friends, actress Terry Moore, in the early fifties.

In my research, Maheu appeared to be the contact that government agencies relied on for the dirty jobs. FBI disclosures have now revealed that no other than J. Edgar Hoover implicated Maheu's involvement in Robert Kennedy's assassination.

In testimony before the U.S. Senate Select Committee on Intelligence in 1975, Maheu defended his role in any assassination scheme as an act of patriotism. The ex-CIA operative used his connection to the hits and his relationship with the Agency to evade legal difficulties. He faced charges for wiretapping Sam Giancana's girlfriend's room. The charges stemmed from Maheu hiring men to bug Phyllis McGuire of the singing McGuire sisters. He told the FBI that he was bugging her to see if she was leaking details about CIA/Mafia hits on Castro.

Many facts remain unclear about Robert Maheu, but some things are certain. Maheu was a paid operative and assassin working for the intelligence wing of the United States Government. He obviously was implementing a specific agenda right from the start, and nothing or nobody was going to get in his way. The fact that the nation's top lawman, J. Edgar Hoover, who Maheu had worked for, believed he orchestrated the Robert Kennedy assassination is quite telling within itself. The distinct possibility exists that Robert Maheu was directly involved in the deaths of Marilyn Monroe and both of the Kennedys. Killing is what he did best. In his twisted view of national security, tying off the loose ends these three represented would have been easy to justify.

Paula Strasberg

In 1955, with the help of Robert Maheu and the FBI, Monroe negotiated a new contract with 20th Century Fox to make four films over seven years. The first film to be made under the deal was "*Bus Stop*," directed by Joshua Logan. In Logan's autobiography "*Movie Stars, Real People and Me*," director Logan wrote:

"I found Marilyn to be one of the great talents of all time. She struck me as being a much brighter person than I had ever imagined, and I think that was the first time I learned that intelligence and, yes, brilliance have nothing to do with education."

During that time, Monroe severed contact with her drama coach, Natasha Lytess, replacing her with Paula Strasberg. During the filming of Monroe's subsequent films, Strasberg would become a constant presence.

Laurence Olivier directed and starred in Marilyn's next film, *"The Prince and the Showgirl."* However, during filming, Olivier resented Monroe's dependence on Paula Strasberg, regarding the coach as a fraud whose only talent was the ability to "butter Marilyn up." He recalled his attempts at explaining a scene to Monroe, only to hear Strasberg interject, "Honey - just think of Coca-Cola and Frank Sinatra."

On one occasion, Arthur Miller remembered Strasberg telling Marilyn: "You are the greatest woman of your time, the greatest human being of your time; of any time, you name it."

With this kind of encouragement from Strasberg, it was easy to see why Marilyn embraced her image.

Blacklisted as a communist by the House Un-American Activities Committee at that time, Paula worked hard to become the only person Marilyn trusted. With Robert Maheu at the controls, Paula also began teaching Marilyn the inner workings of the Communist movement.

Marilyn would learn what information the FBI was looking for and how to get it.

When the relationship between Monroe and Miller was developing, the press began to write about them as a couple. As rumors of their impending marriage began to surface, they became the targets of excessive media interest. They were eventually married on June 29, 1956.

The reports of marriage and romance soon were overshadowed by news that Miller to testify before the House Un-American Activities Committee. They had subpoenaed him to explain his affiliations with communist members of Group Theatre. The Committee ordered him to testify because Maheu and Strasberg convinced Marilyn to get information about Miller's friends and activities. Miller refused to identify any communists and consequently charged with contempt of

Congress. Paula's husband, Lee Strasberg, was a former member of Group Theatre. When they came under fire from the committee, he formed Actors Studio, which was quickly joined by many of the top actors of that time. Although he proclaimed it was not an extension of Group Theatre, the leftist political orientation was undeniable.

According to Marilyn's diary, Miller was urged by the Strasberg to cooperate with the committee through the FBI. However, Miller refused and branded the couple as "snitches." Marilyn's writings also expressed regret for "letting them use her" to set up Miller. During the hearings, she paid many of his legal bills and remained by his side throughout the process. After Arthur Miller won his appeal and filmed "*The Misfits*" with Marilyn, they ended their relationship with the Strasberg and each other.

Dr. Theodore Curphey

My first direct encounter with Dr. Theodore Curphey came only two weeks after being employed by the Los Angeles County Coroner's Office. George Reeves, the actor who played the original "*Superman*," had been found dead. Family members said it murder, and Dr. Curphey was calling it a suicide. Somehow I ended up in the middle.

Welcome to the Los Angeles County Coroner's Office. Only weeks after I arrived, this case had thrust

me into controversy. I had neither the experience nor
authority to question the police about evidence at the
scene. Not even my observations of those who knew
something about the circumstances seemed warranted.

My first interaction with Dr. Curphey went
smoothly, unlike many of the others in the office.
Looking back, if I had questioned him about the Reeves
evidence, Curphey and I would have clashed on this one
as well. During the next two years, we disagreed on
many cases, including Ronald Stokes, Ernie Kovacs, and
other controversial deaths. I guess my attention to detail
didn't allow for County regulations getting ignored.
When they handed me that deputy badge and the book
containing its legal responsibilities, my goal was to
follow the law's letter. That didn't sit well with the office
politics because regulations were viewed like guidelines
rather than law.

Enter the death of Marilyn Monroe. Conspirators
involved in this case never intended for the Coroner's
office to receive Marilyn's body. There was an
orchestrated attempt to prevent this from happening.
Once her body arrived, a cascading chain of events began
to take place. That unfortunately placed Dr. Curphey in
a compromising situation.

On Tuesday, August 7, the day Dr. Thomas
Noguchi performed the autopsy on Marilyn, Dr.
Curphey announced that a massive overdose of
barbiturates was the cause of death. He claimed she had
ingested lethal doses of both Nembutal and Chloral

Hydrate, and either could have killed her. The problem with his statement was that the preliminary toxicology report had found no poison in Marilyn's stomach, and secondary toxicology reports were not complete. No mention of Chloral Hydrate had previously arisen, so how did Dr. Curphey come to these early conclusions?

Curphey then assigned her case to the Suicide Investigation Team, led by a group of doctors from the Suicide Prevention Center. They were an organization co-founded by Dr. Curphey. During my investigation, he told me to provide them with anything they needed. That turned out to be setting up a press conference one week later to announce their findings. On August 17, 1962, a packed room of journalists from around the world learned Marilyn's death was a probable suicide.

After that press conference, Dr. Curphey moved straight ahead with closing Marilyn's case. He ordered me to gather what documents were available, disregard those that weren't, and sign the death certificate. The actions of Dr. Theodore Curphey, while handling the Marilyn Monroe case, constituted a breach of the County Coroner's investigative responsibility and a cover-up of the facts surrounding her death. That was the part of Marilyn's case witnessed first-hand by me.

After retiring from the Los Angeles County Coroner's Office in 1967, Dr. Curphey served as a forensic medicine consultant with the Suicide Prevention Center. As far as I know, he never publicly commented on the truth or anything else about Marilyn's death.

Dr. Ralph Greenson and Dr. Myron Engelberg

One of the most intriguing characters in this story is Marilyn's Psychiatrist Dr. Ralph Greenson. When examining his role in her death, many questions are left unanswered with the lingering feeling that he was much more involved than meets the eye.

Ralph Greenson, born Romeo Greenschpoon, was a prominent psychoanalyst who studied medicine in Switzerland. He was listed as a member of the Communist International Party and was very popular with many Hollywood celebrities. Greenson was introduced to Marilyn Monroe in 1960, not long after she began hanging out with John Kennedy. According to her diary and Bob Slatzer, this introduction came by way of Frank Sinatra during the filming of Arthur Miller's *"The Misfits."*

She wrote in her diary:

"I wonder if Frank knew he was a party member."

Frank Sinatra's name has continued to pop up during my investigation. Sinatra garnered considerable attention due to his alleged personal and professional links with organized crime, including figures such as Sam Giancana. The Federal Bureau of Investigation kept records amounting to 2,403 pages on Sinatra. In relation to Marilyn's case, his alleged Mafia ties may only be equaled by his friendship with John F. Kennedy. During his election campaign, Sinatra was one of Kennedy's biggest fundraisers.

After Sinatra introduced Marilyn to Dr. Greenson, she became his patient. That made Greenson one of the most important Communist operatives in America. He had access to the mind of a woman involved in matters of national security. Greenson, well positioned to gather intelligence from every aspect of Marilyn's life, also placed other key people around her to complete his surveillance.

Greenson recommended Dr. Hyman Engelberg as her primary physician and strongly suggested Marilyn hiring Eunice Murray as her housekeeper. Coincidently, both were members of the Communist Party. Her housekeeper's brother, Churchill Murray, was another person under surveillance by the FBI and the CIA. He introduced Monroe to Cuban diplomats in Mexico City.

Dr. Ralph Greenson, like many of his colleagues at the time, relied heavily on drug therapy for his patients. He routinely ordered prescriptions for barbiturates and tranquilizers. He referred Marilyn to Dr. Engelberg, who prescribed most of the medications Greenson ordered for her.

Marilyn's friends noticed that the more she saw Greenson, the more miserable she became. Jeanne Carmine and Terry Moore described how she deteriorated under Greenson's care, becoming insecure and depressed.

On the night of Marilyn's death, Dr. Greenson was strangely the first doctor called and not her primary physician Dr. Engelberg. According to Greenson, upon his arrival, he broke her bedroom window, climbed through, and did nothing else except removing the phone from her hand. When Jack Clemmons arrived on the scene, Greenson pointed to the empty prescription containers on the table next to her and simply said, "She must have taken all these."

Engelberg, who was described by police as despondent after examining Monroe's body, discussed her battle with manic depression and chemical dependency with the Los Angeles County Coroner and Suicide Investigation Team. Both doctors reportedly told investigators she was suicidal and died as a result of a drug overdose.

At later times, both doctors would recant ever saying Marilyn was suicidal or that they believed her death was suicide. But questions remain as to why they took so long to call the police after discovering her body and why they lied to Police and Coroner's investigators. Perhaps the biggest mystery of all was who prescribed the chloral hydrate that killed Marilyn.

Engelberg told the Los Angeles Times that he had prescribed Nembutal capsules only two or three days before her death and that she was to take one each night to help her sleep. A 50-capsule bottle of the sedative, among some seven or eight other medicine bottles, were all found empty on her nightstand. He also stated that he was surprised to see that many empty containers and that his Nembutal prescription was for only 25 pills. Engelberg claimed he never prescribed any choral hydrate.

Los Angeles County Coroner Theodore J. Curphey said after an autopsy that his "presumptive opinion" was that death was due to an overdose of some drug. He opted not to conduct a formal Inquest. Instead, he appointed a three-member team of mental health professionals to probe into her background. They also concluded her death was a probable suicide. These conclusions were based mainly upon the testimony of Marilyn's doctors.

Whatever Greenson's role in the cover-up of her death, his overall involvement had profound implications.

Monroe knew a great deal about the behind-the-scenes world of American politics. Still, the question remains how much she had told her psychoanalyst.

Being a devout communist, Ralph Greenson wanted all the latest gossip from Marilyn regarding her secret conversations with Robert and John Kennedy. He also had Marilyn record many audiocassettes about her experiences, one of which he shared with former Deputy District Attorney John Miner.

Miner proclaimed on the "*Marilyn Files Live*" television show that he had heard one of the tapes. After listening to its contents, Miner told authorities that he had changed his opinion about her death from suicide to homicide. He promised Greenson that he would never reveal the contents because of confidentiality considerations.

This turned out to be another tape that could have a bearing on solving the mystery of her death. Although we don't know what information it contained, we can be sure it was at least damaging enough to change Miner's mind. The Greenson family may still possess the tape.

At least one investigative writer, Donald Spoto, believes Greenson killed Marilyn, and ambulance driver James Hall has stated the same. My investigation suggests that Dr. Ralph Greenson helped orchestrate this intricate cover-up, but could not have acted alone. He didn't have the political power or clout to implement this master plan. He might have been a bullet, but he didn't shoot the gun.

Incidentally, 20th Century Fox Studios later produced and released a movie based on the life of Dr. Ralph Greenson. He was paid a whopping $250,000 for the film, "Captain Newman M.D.," which portrayed him as an American hero.

Eunice Murray

Hired at Greenson's urging, Eunice Murray was Marilyn's housekeeper. As it turned out, Murray was a trained psychiatric nurse who had worked nearly fifteen years for Greenson. She apparently had been put there to observe Marilyn's reactions to his Psychoanalytic treatments. In the days leading up to Marilyn's death, the actress had become increasingly concerned about

Mrs. Murray. She had begun telling her friends, "There's a spy in my house."

Jeanne Carmine stated that Murray was "sneaky" and always seemed "very suspicious." FBI files also listed Eunice Murray as a card-carrying member of the Communist Party along with her brother, Churchill Murray, who was a member of an open group of American Communists.

The night of Marilyn's death, Eunice Murray changed her story about the timeline of the night's events. According to Jack Clemmons, she first stated that she discovered something was wrong sometime around midnight. Later her story was recanted, saying it wasn't until 3:30 am that she first noticed. During a 1985 BBC interview session with journalist Anthony Summers, he claims Murray reverted to her original story. She broke down in tears saying, "Why do I have to continue lying after all of these years?"

It has always been a mystery to me that she didn't hear the fighting and arguing taking place in the house that evening. Nearly every investigator ever involved in this case, including myself, believes Eunice Murray knew more than she ever told. If officials had subpoenaed her to testify under oath, I'm sure explosive information would have come forth about that fateful night, August 4, 1962. However, just like so many others involved in Marilyn's case, Eunice Murray has taken all of those secrets to the grave. She leaves behind only speculation about what she saw and heard that evening.

The Communist Connection

The subject of Communism may be the single largest reoccurring theme throughout this Marilyn saga. From the time Robert Maheu first contacted her until the moment she died, there was an undeniable communist presence in Marilyn's life. The question is, why?

It is essential to understand that the war between capitalism and socialism was at its peak during Marilyn's lifetime. These opposing political views divided not only our nation but also the entire world. Marilyn was schooled in the ways of communism. However, it wasn't because she was a communist, but rather a weapon in the war.

Marilyn was recruited to spy on Arthur Miller's communist activities, according to her diary. A 34-page FBI report, compiled in 1961, says that an informant identified Miller as being "under Communist Party discipline." The informant also told the FBI, "Miller became disillusioned with the party because the party did not stimulate in him the ability and inspiration to do creative writing, as he had expected when he joined the party." Could these comments have come from Marilyn?

Marilyn's diary and CIA documents both reveal she also attended secret meetings discussing assassination plans for Fidel Castro. What was Marilyn doing there?

Marilyn's diary, and additional intelligence documents, also reveal Marilyn helped bring down Indonesian President, Achmad Sukarno, whose country was allegedly drifting into communist hands. Why was Marilyn selected for this assignment?

Perhaps strangest of all is that both of Marilyn's doctors and her housekeeper were known communists. Marilyn Monroe died with these people watching over her. After her death, they concocted the story of suicide and spread the tale to everybody who would listen. To this day, that is why the ruling of 'probable suicide' is still on Marilyn's death certificate.

CHAPTER 16:
The Closing Argument

I begin this closing argument by saying that my fifty-year experience with the Marilyn Monroe investigation led me to some reasonable conclusions about the killing of this woman. For the majority of those years, I just wanted to understand how she died and why the conspirators set-up me up.

At first glance, when one examines the evidence, these answers seem simple. Somebody obviously gave Marilyn enough drugs to kill her, and I interfered with the cover-up plan. However, under closer examination, a much broader picture begins to emerge.

Marilyn's story represents a time in history when our nation was trying to enter its own modernity. America was still defining its future. Her death, tragic as it was, only served to illustrate a fundamental systemic problem, which has become commonplace in this experiment called American Freedom.

The early 20th Century had laid the foundation for an advanced society ready to reach unlimited potential and become the greatest country on Earth. However, entrenched in this foundation full of promise was a dark side. This iniquity was an untested concept that, without proper monitoring and oversight, could lead to an abuse of power like nothing else. It was called capitalism.

Coming out of World War II, the American workforce was robust, and skilled laborers were at an all-time high. Industrialists such as General Motors, Lockheed, General Electric, DuPont, U.S. Steel, and many other manufacturers were making money hand over fist. However, many laborers were still getting paid meager wages. Thus, enter the Union Movement and the organization of the national labor workforce. During the Second World War, Unions gained significant strength and became involved in every aspect of American labor.

This growth of unions became the single largest threat to the prosperity of big American businesses. Not only did the unions organize the Laborers, but they also utilized the muscle of organized crime to prevent the strikebreaking tactics of the Industrialists. To combat this, corporations turned to politicians who could wield the power of U.S. Government agencies and win back their advantage.

In 1953, Senator Joe McCarthy picked up the banner, devising a plot to create public panic about the threat of communism. McCarthy began targeting every group and organization in opposition to America's capitalism movement. He mounted what became a witch-hunt for American citizen communists. A branch of the United States Government, called The House Un-American Activities Committee, began accusing and prosecuting people who disagreed with the system.

Hollywood writers were among the first groups to fall into this category of communists. Many writers and producers saw the dark side of capitalism. They began creating films and plays that presented negative portrayals of American life. Hollywood's liberal attitude towards socialism and economic equality in America was a problem for the Industrialists' agenda. Play writer Arthur Miller was the most well known name placed on the communist list.

Federal Bureau of Investigation Director J. Edgar Hoover also joined the fight. He called Unions, the Civil Rights Movement, and Liberal Government officials the biggest threat to our country's national security. The war against Communism was now an all-out battle. This scenario is what led to this story's most vulnerable victim, Marilyn Monroe.

Examining Marilyn's early life, it's easy to see why she was susceptible to the world of espionage. Being raised as a foster child and never knowing the security that comes from a loving family, shaped Marilyn's life in numerous ways. Her mother was mentally unstable and had once even stuffed Marilyn in a zipped military duffel bag, trying to abduct her from a foster home.

Although Marilyn's early life was very traumatic, she always dreamed of being a Hollywood star. When Robert Maheu approached her in the mid-1950s, Marilyn thought her career was slipping away. The studio had canceled her contract and was stonewalling the actress. Then, here comes the FBI to save the day.

They make big promises to save her career are made if she agrees to "Do something for America."

Marilyn became a pawn in a high stakes game of chess, and from the moment she began playing, it was only a matter of time before she was taken. After providing evidence against Arthur Miller, not only did her position in Hollywood advance, but she also became a valuable asset for the U.S. intelligence community. Marilyn was the home-court advantage, and she knew exactly how to play the role. So when John Kennedy brought her into those secret meetings with the Central Intelligence Agency and Mafia gangsters, you can believe that all eyes were on her.

In fact, this worked so well that Big Jim O'Connell and the CIA wanted to use her for more sophisticated operations. The war against communism and socialist ideas was already extending far beyond our American borders. Implementation of capitalism was taking place around the world, and any country failing to comply with the wealthiest powers were deemed, communists. This label stigmatized them as the bad guys, and even more importantly, as anti-America.

That allowed for vast resources of money getting spent to undermine and overthrow foreign governments who wouldn't play ball. Fidel Castro in Cuba and Achmad Sukarno in Indonesia are two prime examples of what our intelligence community was doing around the world. But what makes all of this so significant is that agencies were recruiting vulnerable American citizens to do their clandestine bidding.

For nearly seven years, this woman found herself trapped in a world built to devour even the strongest people. The players in this game were powerful, and the prizes for winning were beyond comprehension. Yes, they were more than willing to give Marilyn the fame and fortune she desired, but it came with a price, and Marilyn didn't understand the fine print.

Sometime in the midst of Marilyn's real-life drama, she began documenting her experiences in a diary. Although we can't be sure exactly when she started writing, my best estimate put its origins sometime around 1960.

The big question we must ask is why Marilyn felt the need to write about events, obviously involving matters of national security. Certainly, she was aware there would be consequences if these details were ever made public. In fact, much of what she wrote was cryptic and took many years of research and fortunate coincidence to decipher.

Marilyn wrote names like Iron Bob and Big Jim, which remained mysteries for decades. Only the research of numerous journalists and the advent of today's information superhighway have allowed me to uncover enough information to discover their true identities. The truth of the matter is, for many years, I believed Bob Slatzer was actually Iron Bob. For the first few years of our relationship, I never mentioned seeing that name in her diary and remained slightly leery of his true intentions concerning me. The possibility always existed that he was part of this grand cover-up, but thankfully that never turned out to be the case.

Bob was one of only three other people who have acknowledged reading entries from the same diary that arrived at the Coroner's Office on August 5, 1962. He once told me that Marilyn was just trying to keep track of things, but I believe she was much smarter than most people gave her credit. Marilyn knew she was in way too deep, and she wasn't going down without a fight. Marilyn wrote this journal, and then made sure key friends read parts of the diary to validate its existence. Once that stage was set, she pulled the biggest trick of all by making sure the book was discovered after she was gone.

After examining the evidence and giving this much consideration, I believe Marilyn played a shell game with her diary. During my years of investigation, there have been multiple sightings of diaries allegedly written by Marilyn, none containing the same information I read. Bobby Kennedy and the secret service searched Marilyn's house for it, yet this one was left behind. Marilyn quite possibly wrote in several diaries, with only one arriving at the Coroner's office.

The controversy surrounding Marilyn Monroe's death was never supposed to happen. Everything had already been put in place to guarantee her death get quickly written off as suicide. Both of Marilyn's doctors and her housekeeper were persuaded to make false statements to police investigators. These statements became the basis used to verify her cause of death. With that in hand, detectives at the crime scene released her body to the mortuary. No tests would take place. No toxicology result would show the absence of poison in her stomach. No capsules would be found lodged in her throat. Her body organs would never have had to disappear. Marilyn would have been dead, and there was nothing anyone could have said.

However, as I've said before, something funny happened along the way. A young deputy working the weekend shift that Sunday morning, decided to order Marilyn's body brought to the Coroner's office.

This unexpected event set off a mad scramble to cover up evidence at the highest levels of county, city, and federal government.

What has become even more apparent is that officials at the Los Angeles Police Department, District Attorney's office, and the LA County Coroner were involved. All three agencies forced to conceal evidence. As for the public servants working for these agencies who witnessed the cover-ups and spoke out, they were all thrown to the sharks and discredited in every imaginable way.

Upon looking at this situation even deeper, the realization sets in that none of these agencies ever had a choice of how to handle these circumstances. Who were they going to prosecute, and what witnesses were they going to call? Whose notes were they going to subpoena, and what would they expect U.S. Intelligence agents to say? All roads to prosecution were dead ends, and the people involved were powerful beyond belief.

As one Los Angeles Times reporter said, I was the first to have the nerve to reveal what Marilyn had discussed in her conversations with the Central Intelligence Agency and Federal Bureau of Investigations. Most people have never wanted to believe the complicated circumstances surrounding Marilyn's story, including those who officially investigated her case.

My memoir, which documents a 50-year experience with Marilyn's case, has formed the basis for these final conclusions I am presenting. I've told my story too many times to count since 1962, but never in this much detail. My answers concerning the mishandling of information at the coroner's office have always been consistent. No county official or employee has ever denied what I've said about missing documents or evidence from Coroner's Case #81128.

This takes us to the days leading up to Marilyn's death. Marilyn was preparing to hold a press conference, which would reveal all of her secrets. During my official investigation, I discovered a typewritten press release in her personal property. Although it contained no date or time and appeared incomplete, its intentions were perfectly clear.

The document stated:

<u>Press Release</u>

**Questions and Answers about
Marilyn's Diary of Secrets**
Event: Marilyn Monroe Press Conference

Place: Los Angeles Press Club
Subject: Marilyn Monroe Reveal's It All
Date:
Time:
For Immediate Release

Marilyn was about to reveal it all. Just think about that. Everything she knew about the Kennedys; everything she had done for the Central Intelligence Agency; the Federal Bureau of Investigation; and everything she had heard about Sam Giancana's Mafia Organization. Marilyn was really about to, as she put it, "Blow the lid off the whole damn thing."

In her diary, Marilyn had written that Peter Lawford was begging her to cancel this press conference. Since then, I have discovered that he was not the only one. Marilyn had told many of her closest friends that she was tired of being used by John and Robert Kennedy. She told Bob Slatzer that she had been promised many things and stood by helplessly as those promises turned into betrayal. Bob said that on the Friday before she died, Marilyn had called him saying that she was trying to get in touch with Bobby Kennedy. He wasn't taking her calls, and she told Bob that if she didn't hear from him by Monday, she was going to hold the press conference.

Marilyn's best friend, Jeanne Carmine, was also aware of the press conference. She said Marilyn was holding the press conference because she was angry at how Bobby had cut off their relationship. Carmine speculated that if Bobby would have explained his situation better to Marilyn, that things might have gone smoother. However, Marilyn had a bad taste in her mouth and felt scorned. Carmine said she is confident that Marilyn would have told the press everything, and Bobby Kennedy knew she would too.

Both Jeanne Carmine and Bob Slatzer saw real danger for Marilyn ahead and warned her about it. None of this mattered to her, and ultimately she may have made the biggest mistake of her life. One week before dying, Marilyn decided to attend one of Frank Sinatra's parties in Lake Tahoe. While there, in a drunken state of mind, she began telling partygoers about the press conference she was planning. Those in attendance included Sam Giancana and Jimmy Hoffa, who both initiated their own wiretap on Marilyn's house. The following Saturday night, they would record the infamous fight between Marilyn and Bobby. The next day she was found dead.

In 1982, the last official public inquiry into Marilyn Monroe's death was held. Los Angeles County Assistant District Attorney Ronald Carroll headed the investigation. In his final report, Carroll stated,

"Our investigators reviewed the 20-year-old results of Dr. Theodore Curphey's coroner's investigation. They were proclaimed to be accurate, and we stand behind the Suicide Investigation Team's findings."

Carroll went on to say, "Marilyn's doctors declared in their professional opinion that she was not in a state of mind to write anything constructive."

He found no evidence that Marilyn's book was ever in the Coroner's Office despite multiple accounts to the contrary.

Often I wondered why Carroll, who had worked hard to get where he was, would so blatantly ignore undeniable facts staring him in the face. But again, what choice did he have? Ron Carroll was a civil service worker just as Jack Clemmons, John Miner, and myself. The only difference was that he knew the rules: play ball or suffer the consequences.

Carroll's boss, Los Angeles County District Attorney John Van De Kamp, would imply that we had made this all up. Why would he think we had nothing better to do than lie to county officials while seeking to testify under oath to the grand jury?

As it turns out, there was never a serious attempt to discover the truth during this investigation. The District Attorney had based all its conclusions on witnesses who were either lying or involved in this cover-up.

Dr. Ralph Greenson, whose professional opinion was the basis of the report, had died in 1978 before the inquiry began. By then, however, Greenson had already recanted his belief that Marilyn was suicidal, according to Deputy District Attorney John Miner. Carroll disregarded this vital information and decided not to use Miner's statements in his final report.

Miner was not the only witness whose testimony was disregarded. Jeanne Carmine also told investigators about reading Marilyn's diary. She also told them about Marilyn's relationship with Bobby Kennedy and her threats about going public with national security matters.

Jack Clemmons, the first police officer on the scene, testified that witnesses had changed their stories about the night's events.

District Attorney investigators ignored him, ultimately omitting any information that conflicted with the original Coroner's findings.

In all, three public officials, representing the Coroner's Office, District Attorney's Office, and Police Department testified during this inquiry about Marilyn's case. However, Van De Kamp and his investigation team cast them all aside.

Recent Government disclosures have now established Marilyn's involvement with the intelligence community. It is my belief this had something to do with her death.

Our federal government knows the answer to this web of deceit. Only the Freedom of Information Act appeal-process shows any hope of answering the call of the people. In that regard, writing this book has been a powerful experience. My research proves that more revealing information exists. A debate is underway in the CIA's Agency Release Panel, concerning whether to release existing documents on Marilyn Monroe. It seems strange for the CIA to debate itself over releasing these documents because, since the beginning, the Agency has claimed to have no records regarding Marilyn Monroe. However, as we know, information to the contrary has continued to surface over the years. When the CIA's hand has been forced, new documents always pop up.

It seems that modern-day bureaucrats are determining what information gets released to the American public. Given what is now known about their complicity in Marilyn's death and the deaths of the other people who are a part of this story, it must be some incriminating information. I remember reading what J. Edgar Hoover said to a friend when told of the Robert Kennedy assassination; "I know that the CIA and their hitman Robert Maheu did it, and there is nothing I can do about it."

I once heard a professor from the University of California say,

"It's Not Truth Until Its Written Down."

If you still don't understand why this story has lasted for 50 years, after you've read this account of Marilyn Monroe's death, I haven't done a good job explaining it. This story has been about a massive cover-up where powerful government officials conspired to hide the truth from the American Public. It is a bold example of how bureaucrats wield their power without any regard for American citizens and lack the desire to tell the truth.

I've given plenty of thought to what national security issues could explain why one of these agencies has never come forward with the details. I believe the answer is simple; it involves the assassination of one of our Presidents and a U.S. Senator. That alone may keep this case a mystery forever.

In closing, let me add a little tidbit. My co-author and researcher has nudged my side since the start, to state my opinion about this case. He told me, "No sane person would compile this kind of data without any conclusion about who killed Marilyn Monroe, or if she committed suicide. You are the only one still alive, who was there when the investigation began. Step out on a limb. Tell us who did it."

My response to him was that I was only looking for her cause of death. I was a Coroner's investigator, not a policeman. My thoughts were that once we found out how she died, it would be easy to conclude whom, if anybody, carried out this plot to silence Marilyn. After 50 years, the list of suspects is more extensive than ever. The elaborate cover-up of evidence that could solve this case is still ongoing.

I close with a word to Marilyn.

On August 6th, 1962, when I walked into the autopsy room and saw you lying on that gurney, the only thought that went through my mind was that your lifestyle had certainly aged you. Your body looked tired and beaten down, but now I understand what you had been through. I hope this book reveals what you wanted to the American public. I tried to do it some justice. In my eyes, you will always twinkle.

Samir

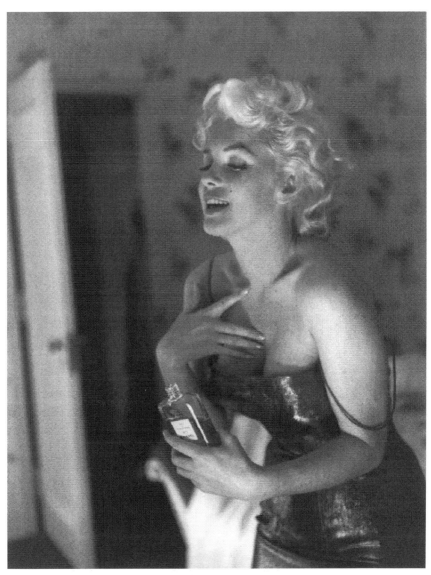

Marilyn Monroe - 1955 (photo by Ed Feingersh)

Marilyn Monroe at party, 1955 (photo uncredited)

Photo of Marilyn Monroe and Arthur Miller at the April in Paris Ball
held at New York's Waldorf-Astoria in 1957. (Associated Press)

Marilyn Monroe posing below an Actors Studio sign in May 1961

Lionel Grandison marries his San Fernando High School sweetheart Alithra Craig in 1958

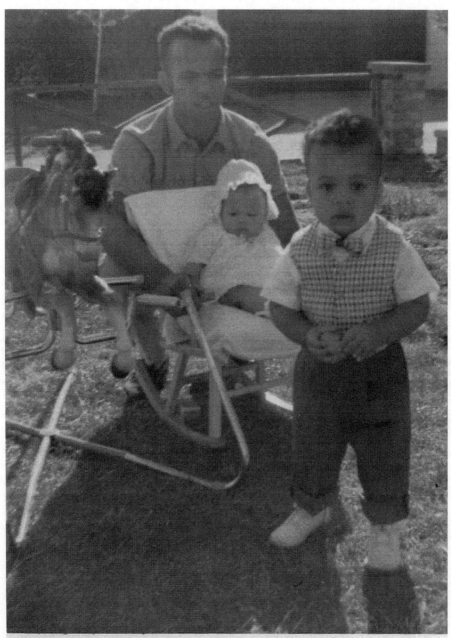

21-year-old Deputy Coroner's Aide Lionel Grandison spends Easter at home with his son Lionel Jr. and daughter Crystal in April of 1961

CERTIFICATE OF DEATH
STATE OF CALIFORNIA—DEPARTMENT OF PUBLIC HEALTH

LOCAL REGISTRATION
DISTRICT NO. 7053   17716

Marilyn	Monroe	August 5, 1962 3 A.
Female Cauc.	Los Angeles, Calif. June 1, 1926	36
unk. unk.	Gladys Pearl Baker —Mexico	United States 565-32-0764
Actress 20	20th Century-Fox	Motion Pictures
none	Divorced	

12305 –5th Helena Drive

Los Angeles   Los Angeles

12305 –5th Helena Drive   Mrs. Inez C. Melson

Los Angeles   Los Angeles   Calif.   9110 Sunset Blvd.

By Lionel Grandison

autopsy   HALL OF JUSTICE LOS ANGELES   8-28-62

Entombment Aug.8,1972   Westwood Memorial Park

Westwood Village Mortuary

ACUTE BARBITURATE POISONING

INGESTION OF OVERDOSE

Probable Suicide   As Above

Home   Los Angeles   L.A.   Calif.

This is a true certified copy of the record
if it bears the seal of the County Recorder
imprinted in purple ink.

FEE
$2.00   SEP 24 1964

Ray E. Lee COUNTY RECORDER
AND DEPUTY COUNTY RECORDER OFFICER
LOS ANGELES COUNTY, CALIFORNIA

Copy of Marilyn Monroe's Death Certificate signed by Coroner's Deputy Lionel Grandison

Los Angeles Police Department
FOLLOW-UP REPORT

☐ MULTIPLE REPORTS   DR 62-509 463

TYPE CRIME
DEATH REPORT

ADDITIONAL MAJOR CRIMES COMMITTED—THIS INCIDENT

DATE AND TIME OCCURRED	DATE AND TIME OF THIS REPORT	LOCATION OF OCCURRENCE	RPTG. DIST.
8-4/5-62 8P/3:35A	8-6-62 4:15P	12305 Fifth Helena Dr.	814

VICTIM'S NAME (as listed on orig. report)	LIC. NO. INVOLVED VEHICLE	CONNECTING PROPERTY REPORTS
MONROE, Marilyn		

| Property Recovery | | TOTAL | PARTIAL | NONE | Additional Property | | LOSS | THIS REPORT | $ |
| Property Disposition | | BOOKED | RELEASED BY DEPT. | | | | RECOVERY | | $ |

| Case Status | REPORT UNFOUNDED | CLEARED | ☐ RECLASSIFY TO: | MAINTAIN WANTS IN PROPERTY FILE? | YES |
| | COMPLAINT REFUSED | X INVEST. CONT. | | | NO |

| PERSON(S) ARRESTED | LA OR "J" NO. | SEX | DESC. | AGE | HGT. | WGT. | HAIR | EYES | HTA DATE | CHARGE | CRT. DIV. |

(1) EXPLAIN INVESTIGATION PROGRESS AND STATUS. (2) DESCRIBE ANY CHANGE IN M.O. (3) WHEN VICTIM AND/OR WITNESSES LISTED IN CRIME REPORT HAVE NOT BEEN INTERVIEWED, GIVE REASON. (4) IF ADDITIONAL PROPERTY LOSS INVOLVED, ITEMIZE, DESCRIBE AND SHOW VALUE, LISTING ALL SERIAL NUMBERS. IF PARTIAL RECOVERY, LIST PROPERTY RECOVERED, USING ITEM NUMBER, DESCRIPTION (SERIAL NO., MONOGRAMS, ETC.) AND VALUE AS IT APPEARS ON INITIAL REPORT. EXPLAIN ANY CHANGES FOUND NECESSARY IN PROPERTY DESCRIPTIONS. REPORT ALL SERIAL NUMBERS AND INSCRIPTIONS DEVELOPED DURING INVESTIGATION.

| ITEM NO. | PERSON REPORTING OR ADDITIONAL PERSONS INTERVIEWED | RESIDENCE ADDRESS | CITY | RESIDENCE PHONE | BUSINESS PHONE |

Upon reinterviewing both Dr. Ralph P. Greenson (Wit #1 and Dr. Hyman Engelberg (Wit #2) they both agree to the following time sequence of their actions.

Dr. Greenson received a phone call from Mrs Murray (reporting person) at 3:30A, 8-5-62 stating that she was unable to get into Miss Monroe's bedroom and the light was on. He told her to pound on the door and look in the window and call him back. At 3:35A, Mrs Murray called back and stated Miss Monroe was laying on the bed with the phone in her hand and looked strange. Dr. Greenson was dressed by this time, left for deceased residence which is about one mile away. He also told Mrs Murray to call Dr. Engelberg.

Dr. Greenson arrived at deceased house at about 3:40A. He broke the window pane and entered through the window and removed the phone from her hand.

Rigor Mortis had set in. At 3:50A, Dr. Engelberg arrived and pronounced Miss Monroe dead. The two doctors talked for a few moments. They both believe that it was about 4A when Dr. Engelberg called the Police Department.

A check with the Complaint Board and WLA Desk, indicates that the call was received at 4:25A. Miss Monroe's phone, GR 61890 has been checked and no toll calls were made during the hours of this occurrence Phone number 472-4830 is being checked at the present time.

If additional space is required, use Continuation Sheet, Form 2730	TOTAL VALUE $
DATE AND TIME TYPED	DIVISION	CLERK	INTERVIEWING OFFICER(S)	SER. NO.	DIVISION	PERSON REPORTING (SIGNATURE)
8-6-62 10:25A WLA JE			R E BYRON 2730 WLA D			X

FOLLOW-UP REPORT

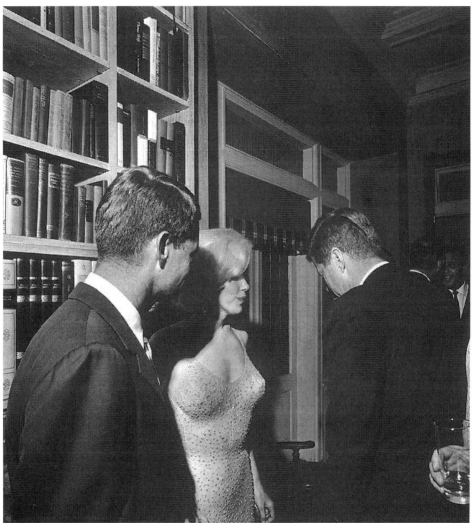

U.S. President John F. Kennedy (right), U.S. Attorney General Robert Kennedy (left), and actress Marilyn Monroe, on the occasion of President Kennedy's 45th birthday celebrations at Madison Square Garden in New York City.. - April, 1962

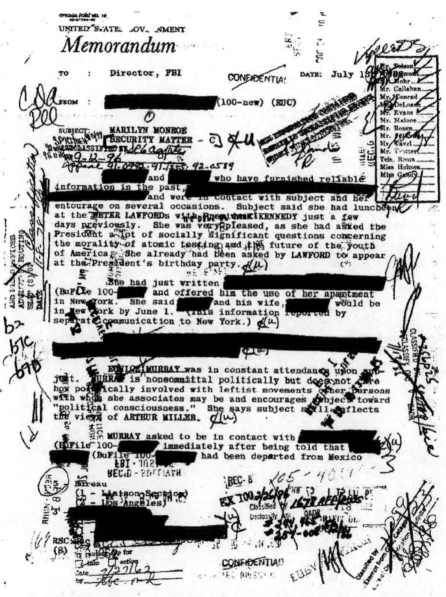

Declassified FBI disclosures that include the names of Marilyn Monroe, John F. Kennedy, Arthur Miller, Eunice Murray, and Peter Lawford.

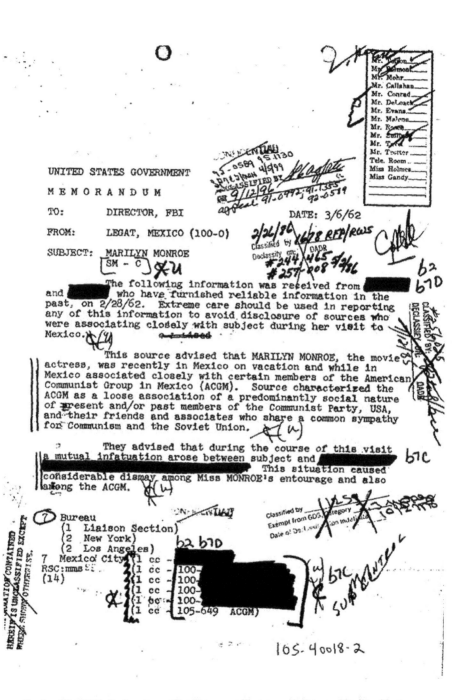

UNITED STATES GOVERNMENT

M E M O R A N D U M

TO: DIRECTOR, FBI   DATE: 3/6/62

FROM: LEGAT, MEXICO (100-0)

SUBJECT: MARILYN MONROE
           [SM - C]

The following information was received from
and ▮▮▮▮ who have furnished reliable information in the
past, on 2/28/62. Extreme care should be used in reporting
any of this information to avoid disclosure of sources who
were associating closely with subject during her visit to
Mexico.

This source advised that MARILYN MONROE, the movie
actress, was recently in Mexico on vacation and while in
Mexico associated closely with certain members of the American
Communist Group in Mexico (ACGM). Source characterized the
ACGM as a loose association of a predominantly social nature
of present and/or past members of the Communist Party, USA,
and their friends and associates who share a common sympathy
for Communism and the Soviet Union.

They advised that during the course of this visit
a mutual infatuation arose between subject and ▮▮▮▮▮▮▮
▮▮▮▮▮▮▮▮▮▮▮▮ This situation caused
considerable dismay among Miss MONROE's entourage and also
among the ACGM.

⑦ Bureau
   (1 Liaison Section)
   (2 New York)
   (2 Los Angeles)
7 Mexico City (1 cc -
RSC:mms   (1 cc - 100-
(14)   (1 cc - 100-
             (1 cc - 100-
             (1 cc - 100-
             (1 cc - 105-649 ACGM)

165-40018-2

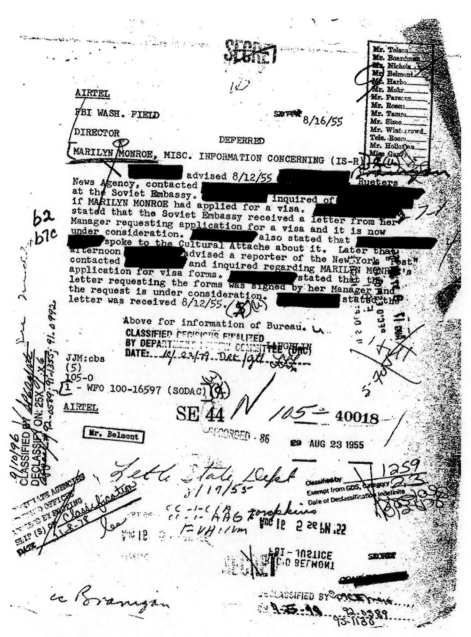

Declassified FBI disclosures regarding Marilyn Monroe's application for a travel visa to the Soviet Union

Lionel Grandison at KPOL Radio on Sunset Blvd in Hollywood. This studio is where he first met Robert Slatzer in 1974, while producing public affairs programming for Capital Cities Communications.

Samir Muqaddin (Lionel Grandison) signs a commissioned art rendering of Marilyn Monroe and himself created by internationally-acclaimed fine artist, Jameel Rasheed.

"The Case of Marilyn Monroe" art unveiling. From the left, Lionel Grandison II, Samir Muqaddin (Lionel Grandison), Artist Jameel Rasheed, Lionel Grandison Jr.

Academy Award-winning Actor Louis Gossett Jr. invited Samir Muqaddin to come visit him at his private ranch estate in Malibu in 2014.

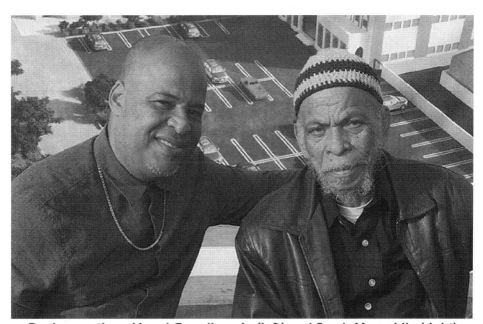

Book co-authors Lionel Grandison Jr. (left) and Samir Muqaddin (right)
(November 2018)

CHAPTER 18:
Obituary

Samir Abdul Muqaddin, birth name Lionel Alfred Grandison, was born on February 16, 1940, at Charity Hospital in New Orleans. At the age of one, his family moved west to North Hollywood, California, where he attended school at Lankershim Elementary and, for a short while, North Hollywood High.

The family later purchased a home in the Los Angeles suburb of Pacoima, where he began attending San Fernando High School. While there, Lionel, who was given the nickname "Frenchy" because of his family's Louisiana heritage, met his future bride-to-be, Alithra "Tipy" James. After graduation, they would marry and produce three children, Lionel Jr., Crystal Arlene, and Lance Alvin.

In 1975, Lionel Grandison Sr. changed his name to Samir Muqaddin after embracing the religion of Islam. He became a successful businessman and prominent member of the Los Angeles Muslim community.

His company, Baitcal Media Group, has contributed heavily to building a new multi-million-dollar Islamic Center, located on the corner of Martin Luther King Blvd and Central Ave near downtown LA.

Samir passed away on January 6, 2021, from COVID-19. He is survived by his three children, 12 grandchildren, five great-grandchildren, and a host of family and friends who miss him dearly.

"From God we come, and to Him we return"

Samir Abdul Muqaddin (Lionel Grandison Sr.)   2/16/40 – 1/6/2021